D1328602

TUNDRA

© 2011 Chad Carpenter

All Rights reserved. No part of this book may be reproduced or transmitted in any form by any means, electronic or mechanical, including photocopying, recording, or by any information storage and retrieval system, without written permission from the Publisher.

Published by Willow Creek Press, Inc.
P.O. Box 147, Minocqua, Wisconsin 54548

Printed in China

TUNDRA
WET, WILD & WEIRD

CHAD CARPENTER

Willow Creek Press®

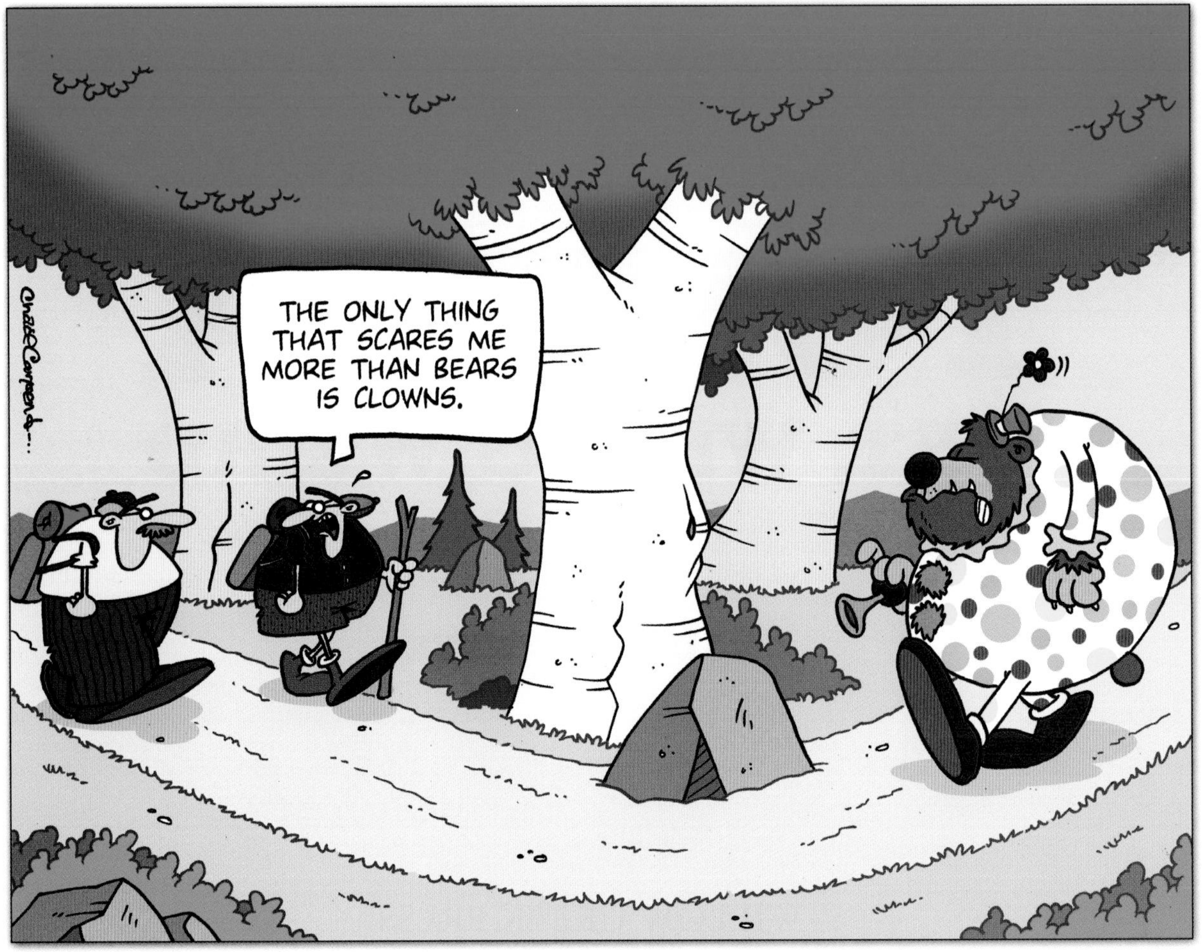
THE ONLY THING THAT SCARES ME MORE THAN BEARS IS CLOWNS.

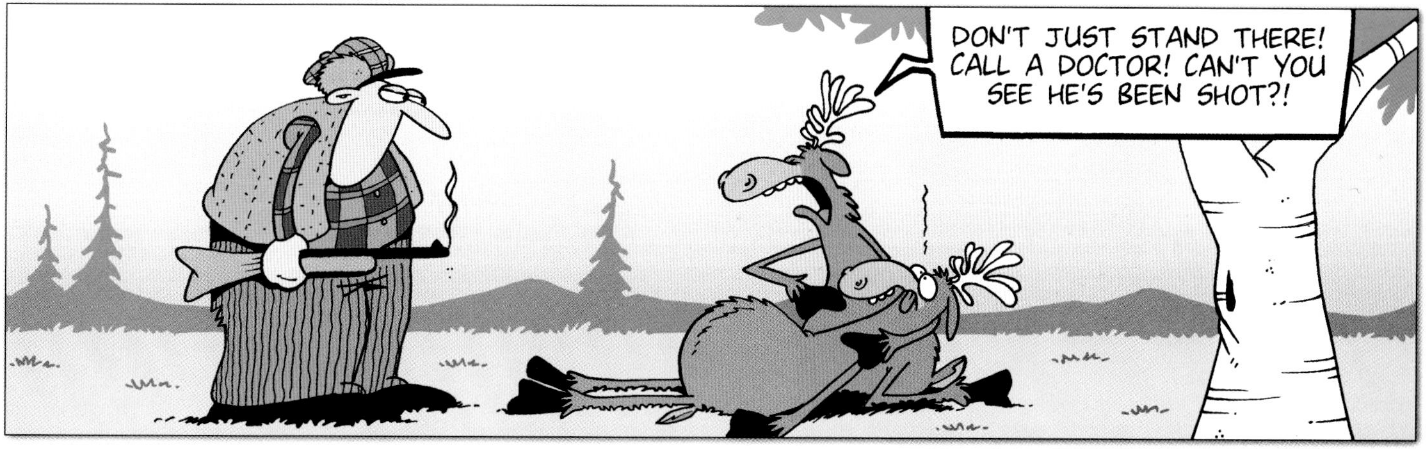
DON'T JUST STAND THERE! CALL A DOCTOR! CAN'T YOU SEE HE'S BEEN SHOT?!

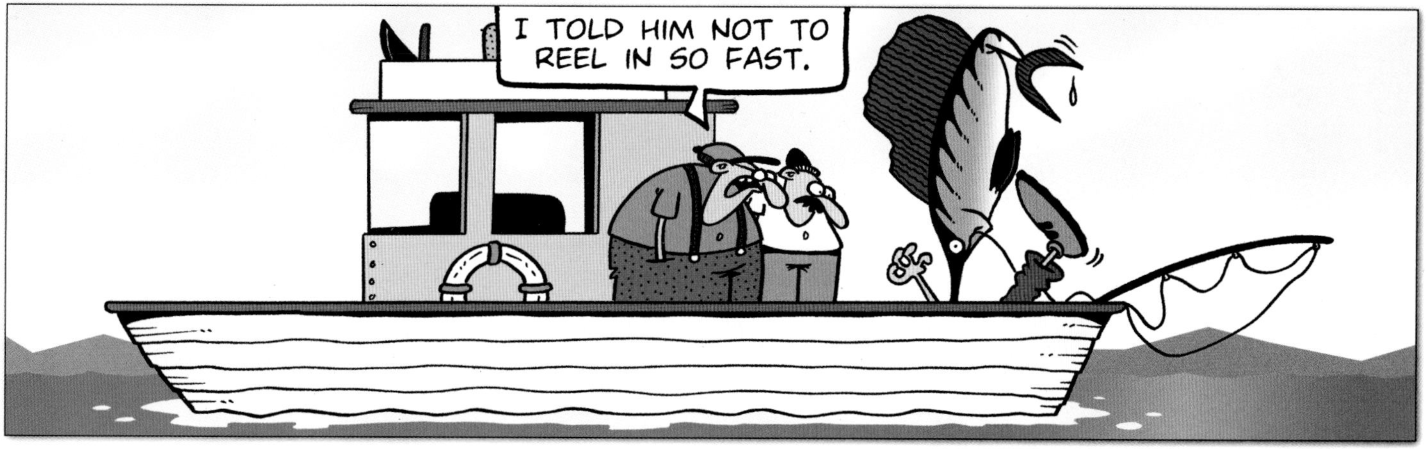
I TOLD HIM NOT TO REEL IN SO FAST.

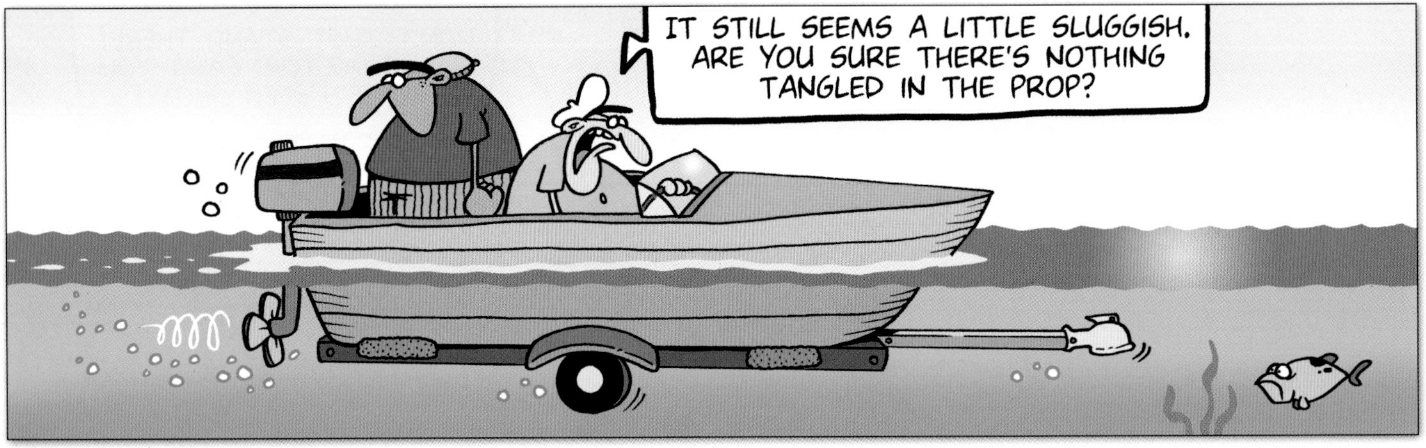
IT STILL SEEMS A LITTLE SLUGGISH. ARE YOU SURE THERE'S NOTHING TANGLED IN THE PROP?

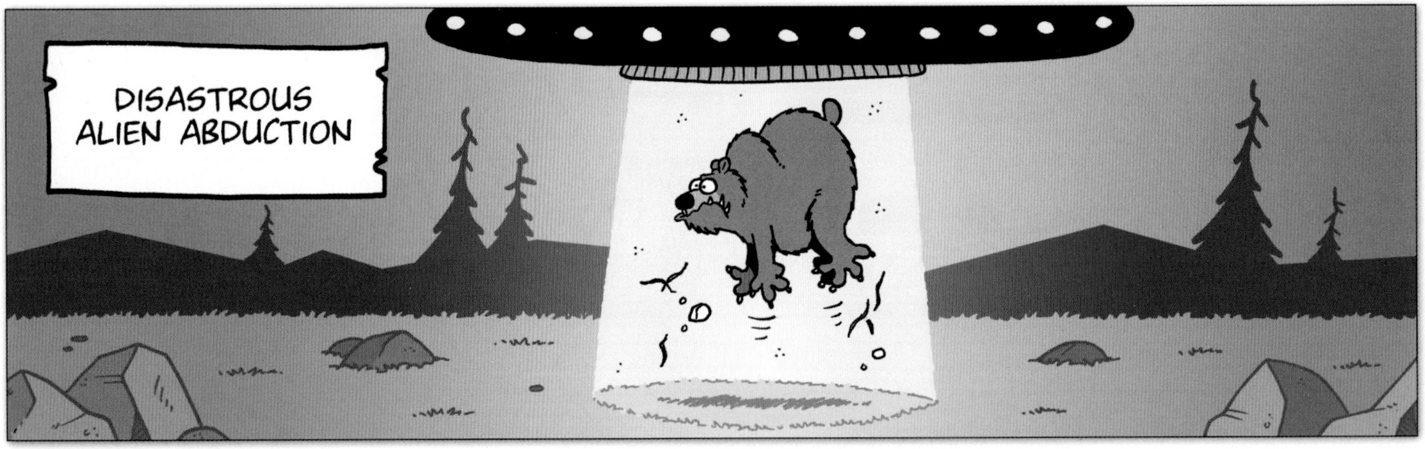
DISASTROUS ALIEN ABDUCTION

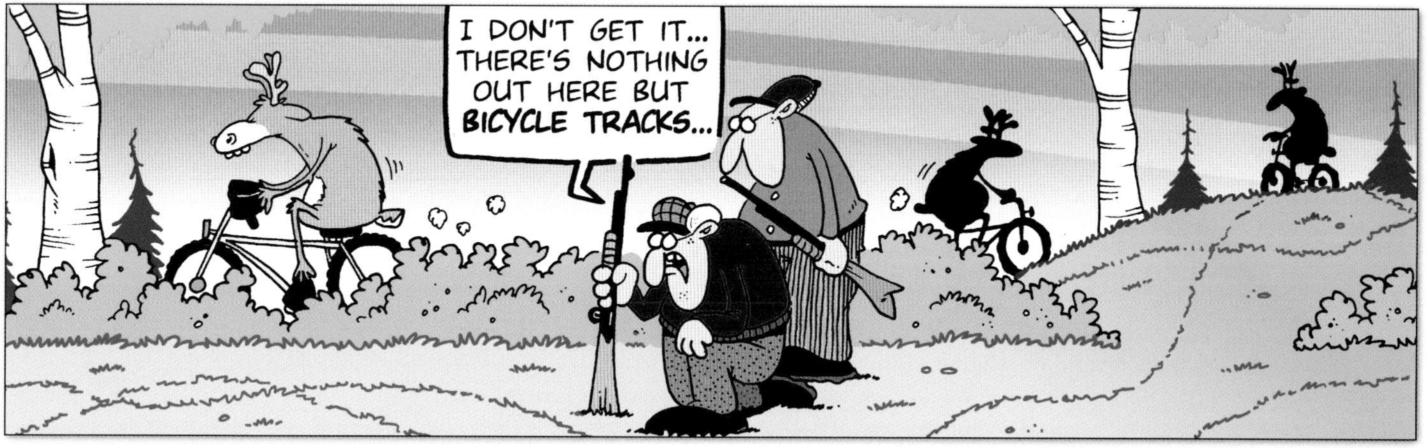
I DON'T GET IT... THERE'S NOTHING OUT HERE BUT **BICYCLE TRACKS...**

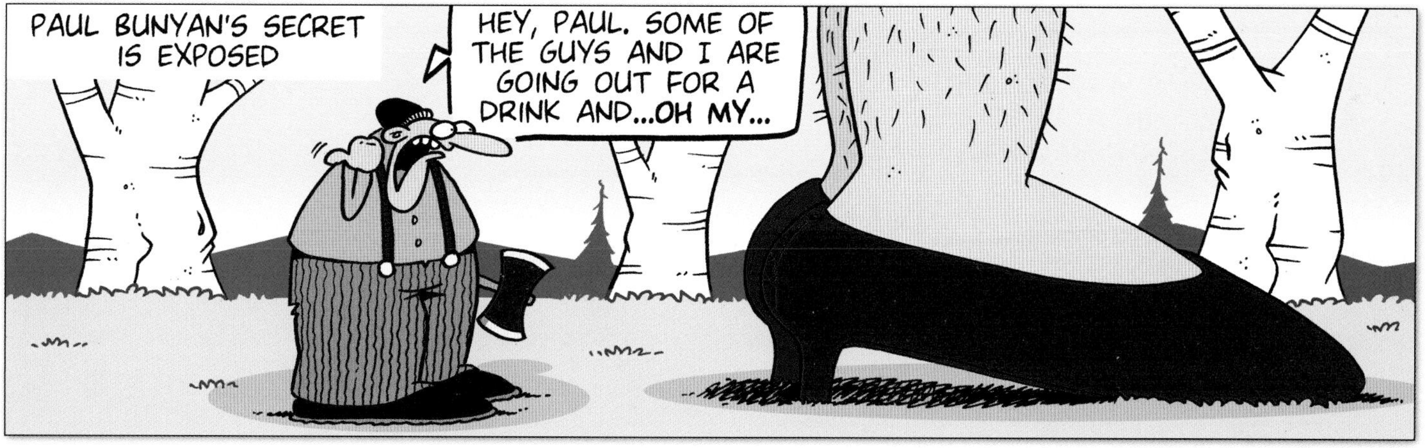
PAUL BUNYAN'S SECRET IS EXPOSED
HEY, PAUL. SOME OF THE GUYS AND I ARE GOING OUT FOR A DRINK AND...OH MY...

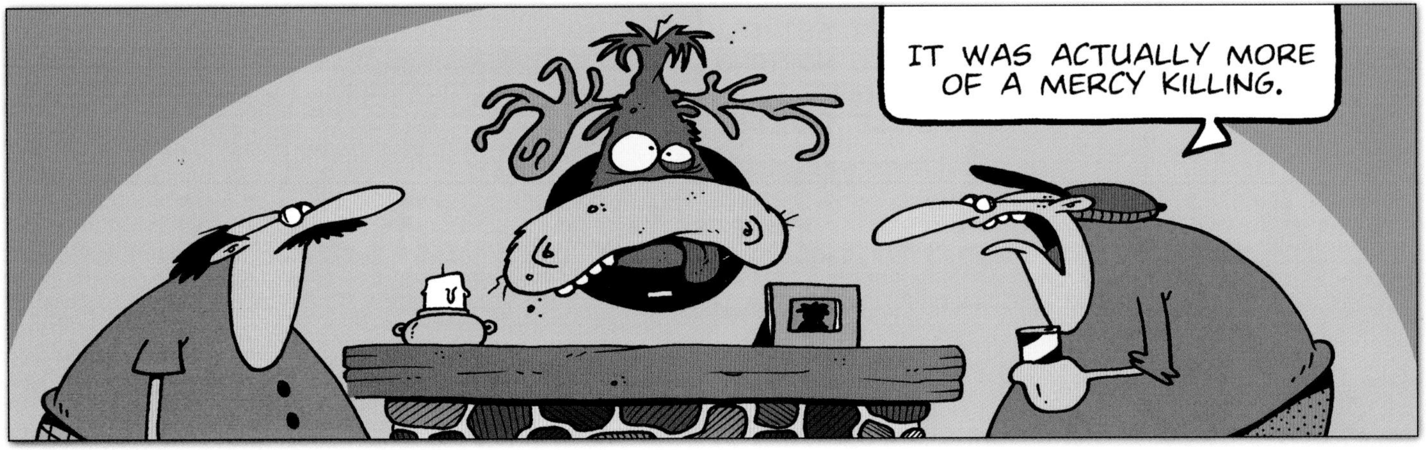
IT WAS ACTUALLY MORE OF A MERCY KILLING.

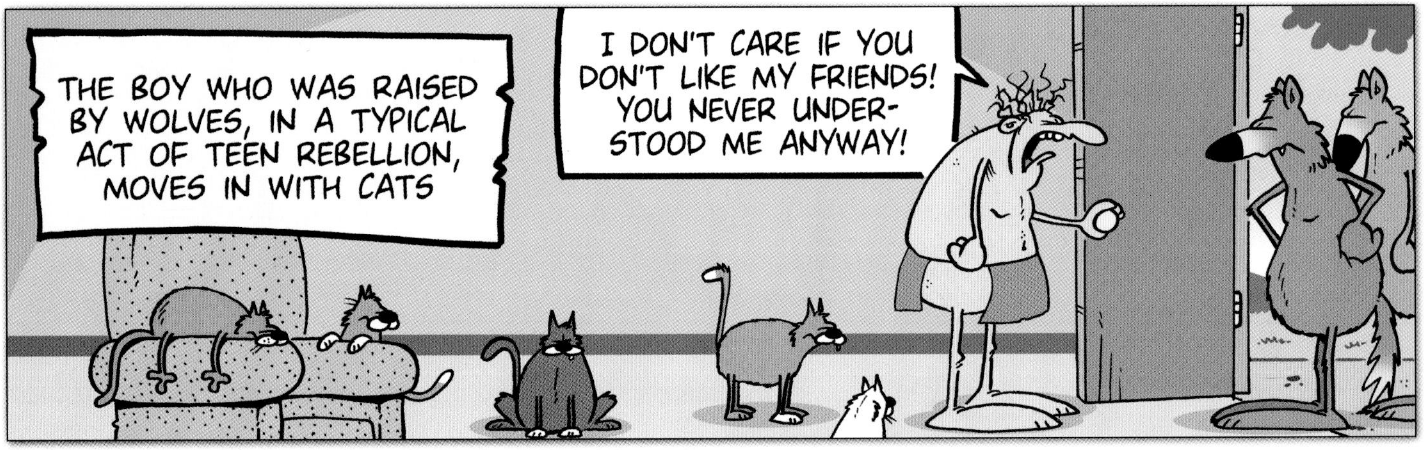
THE BOY WHO WAS RAISED BY WOLVES, IN A TYPICAL ACT OF TEEN REBELLION, MOVES IN WITH CATS
I DON'T CARE IF YOU DON'T LIKE MY FRIENDS! YOU NEVER UNDER-STOOD ME ANYWAY!

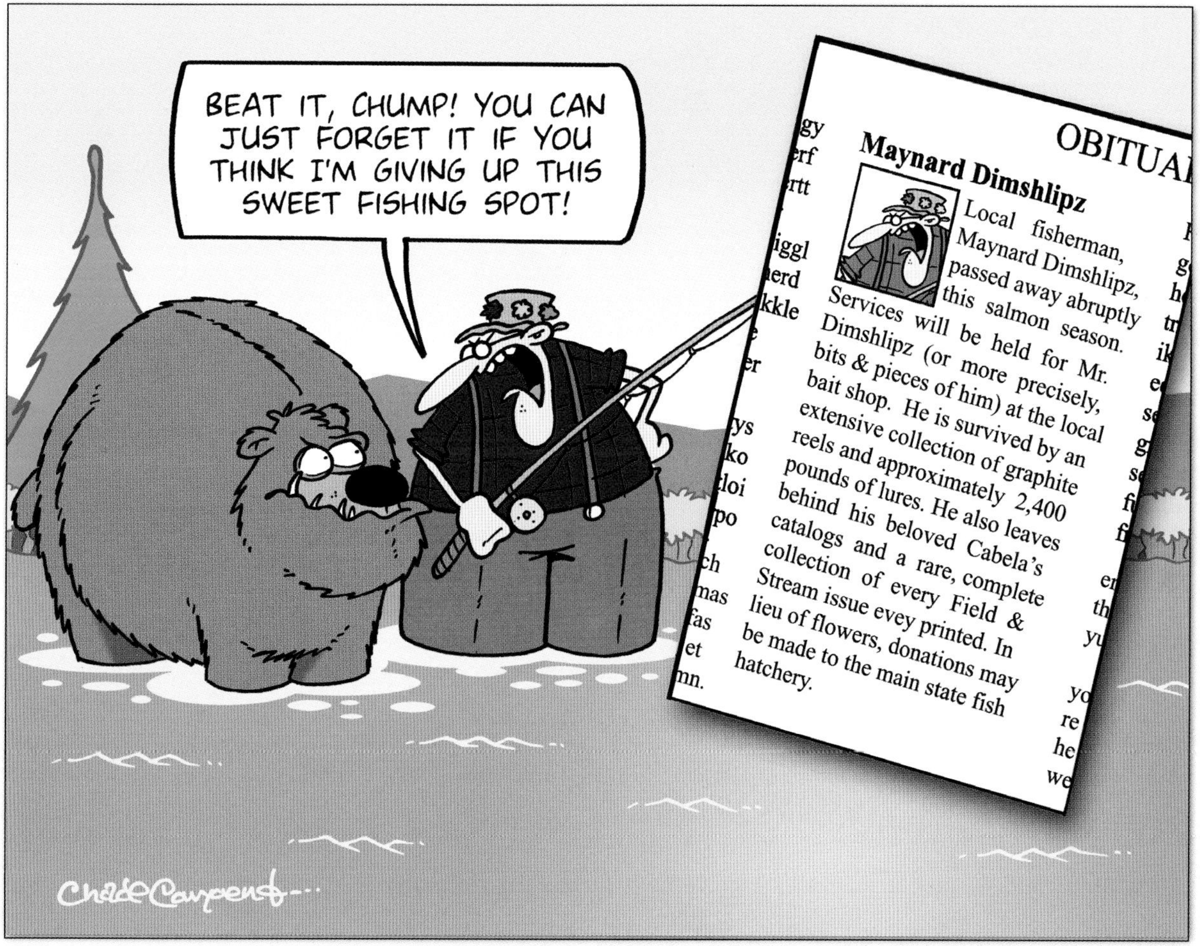
BEAT IT, CHUMP! YOU CAN JUST FORGET IT IF YOU THINK I'M GIVING UP THIS SWEET FISHING SPOT!
Maynard Dimshlipz
Local fisherman, Maynard Dimshlipz, passed away abruptly this salmon season. Services will be held for Mr. Dimshlipz (or more precisely, bits & pieces of him) at the local bait shop. He is survived by an extensive collection of graphite reels and approximately 2,400 pounds of lures. He also leaves behind his beloved Cabela's catalogs and a rare, complete collection of every Field & Stream issue evey printed. In lieu of flowers, donations may be made to the main state fish hatchery.

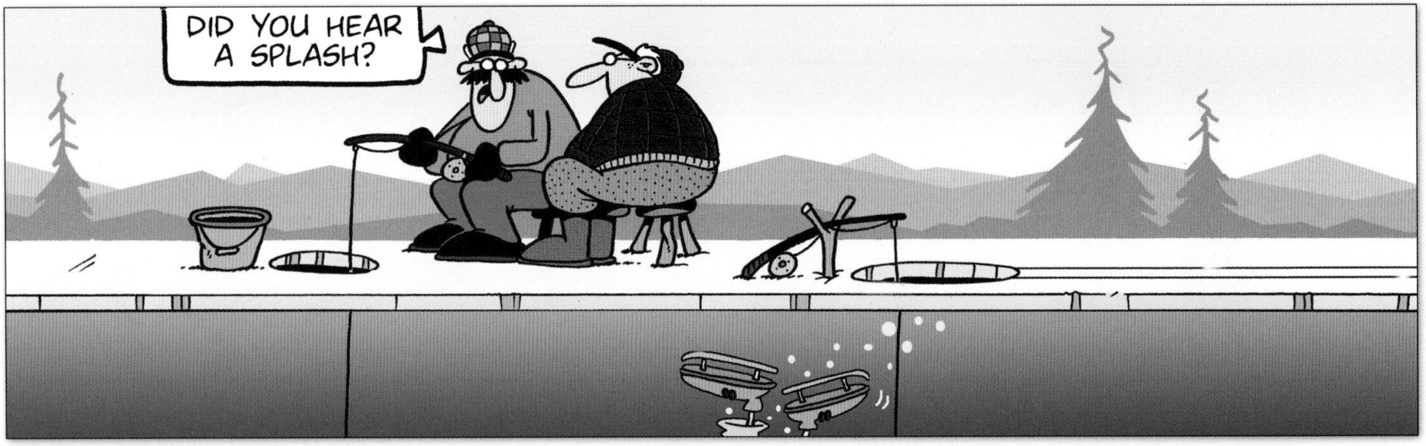
DID YOU HEAR A SPLASH?

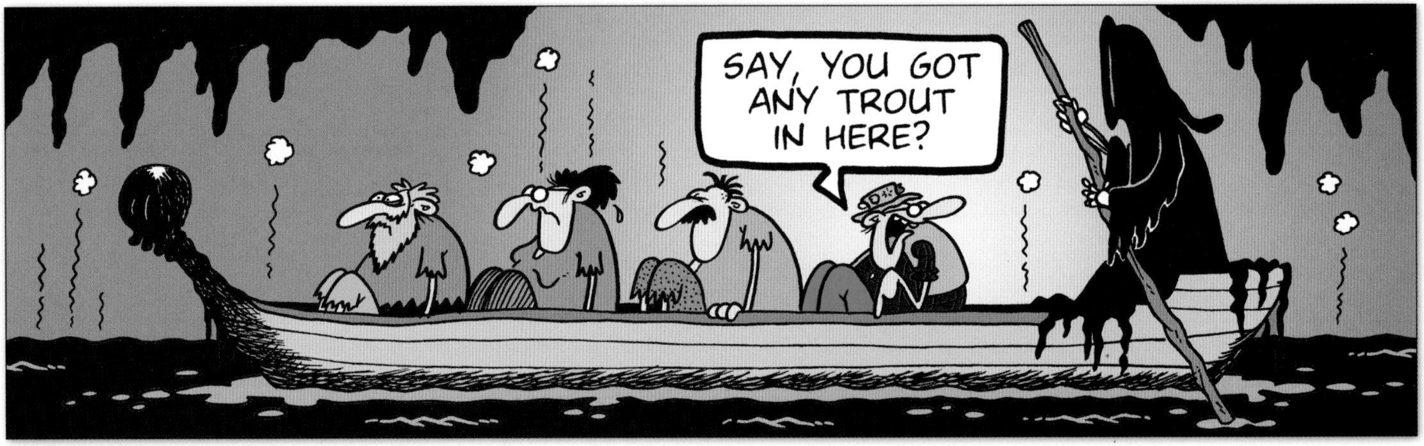
SAY, YOU GOT ANY TROUT IN HERE?

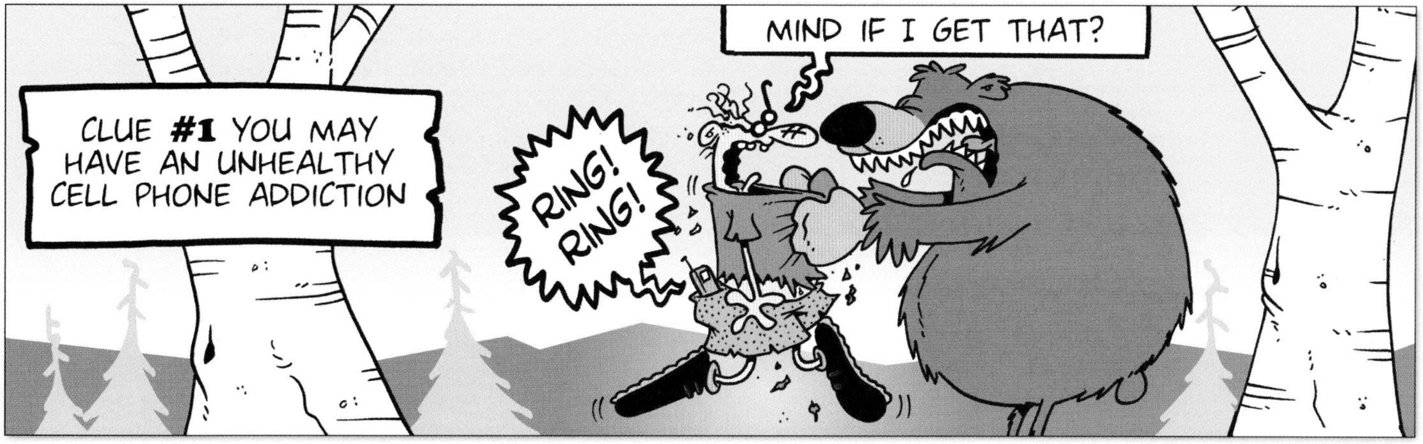
CLUE #1 YOU MAY HAVE AN UNHEALTHY CELL PHONE ADDICTION
RING! RING!
MIND IF I GET THAT?

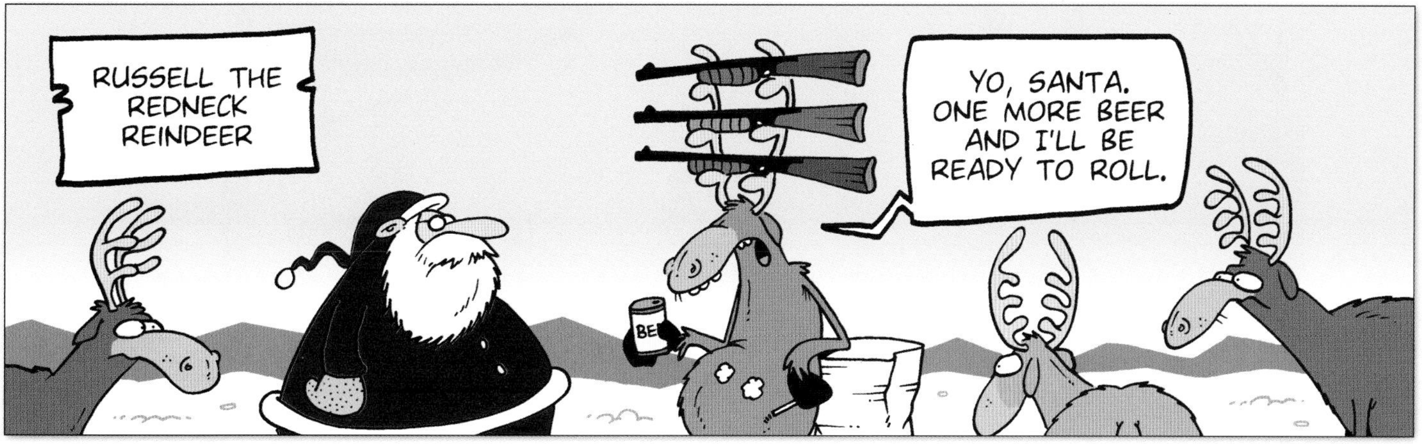
RUSSELL THE REDNECK REINDEER
YO, SANTA. ONE MORE BEER AND I'LL BE READY TO ROLL.

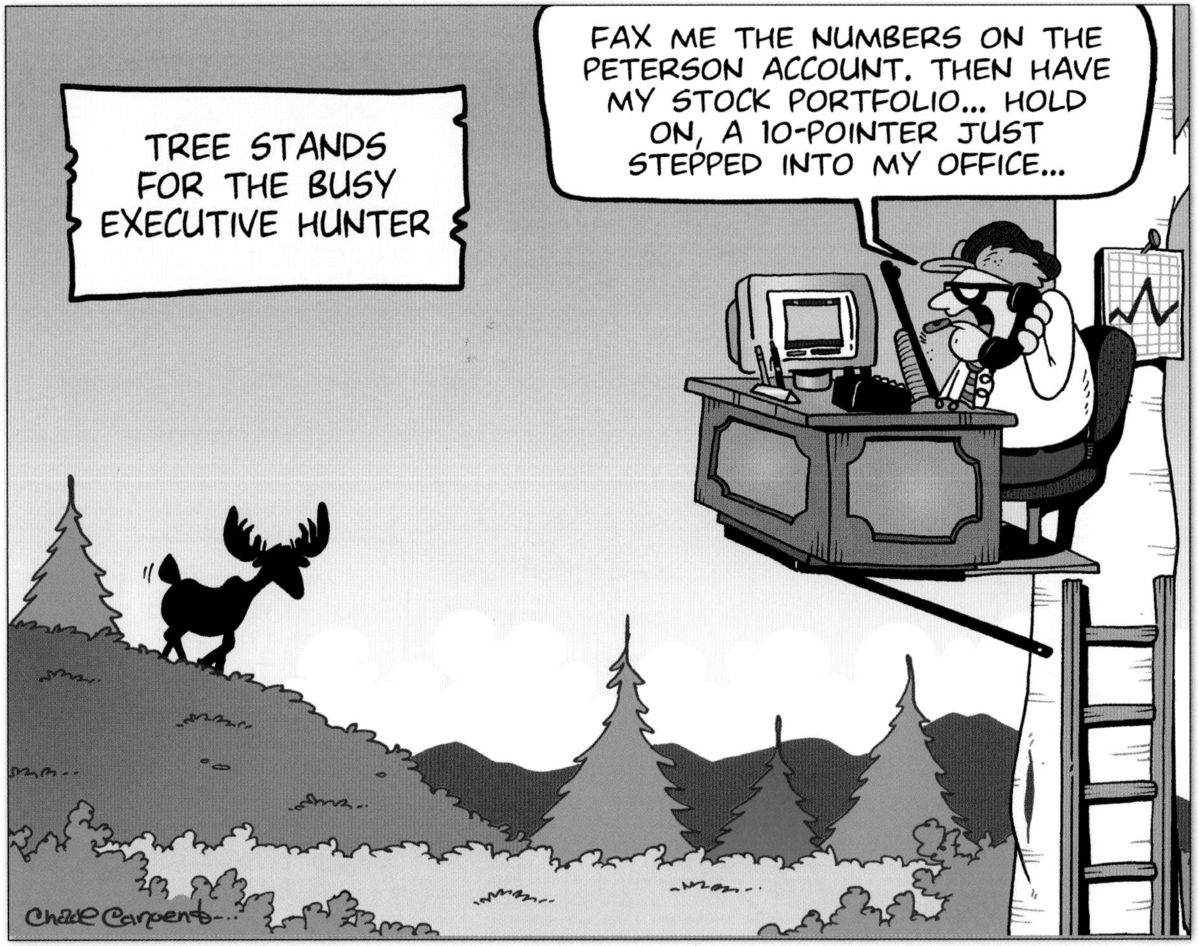
TREE STANDS FOR THE BUSY EXECUTIVE HUNTER
FAX ME THE NUMBERS ON THE PETERSON ACCOUNT. THEN HAVE MY STOCK PORTFOLIO... HOLD ON, A 10-POINTER JUST STEPPED INTO MY OFFICE...
Chade Carpenter

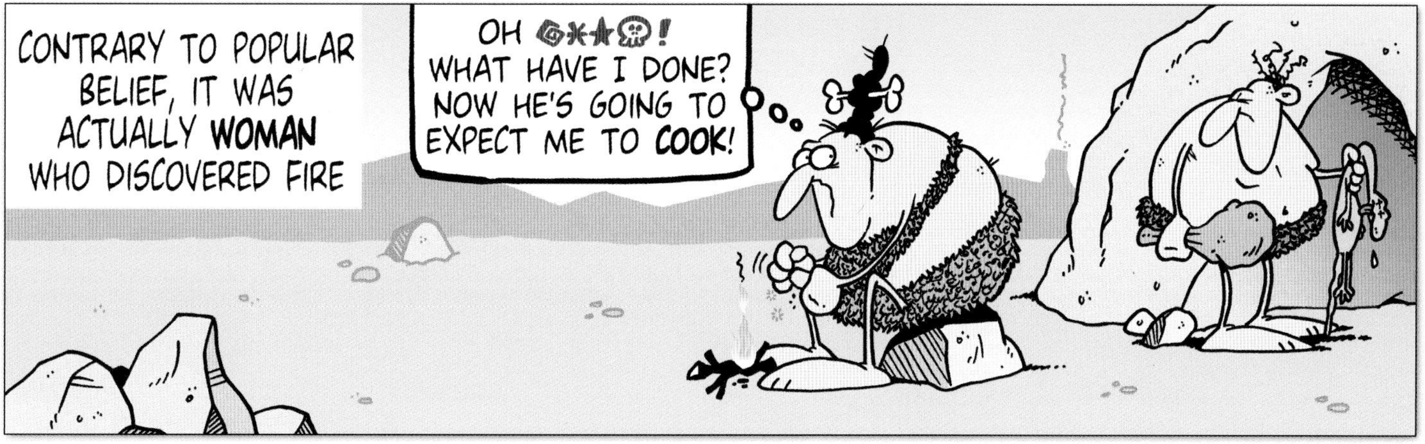
CONTRARY TO POPULAR BELIEF, IT WAS ACTUALLY **WOMAN** WHO DISCOVERED FIRE
OH !
WHAT HAVE I DONE? NOW HE'S GOING TO EXPECT ME TO **COOK**!

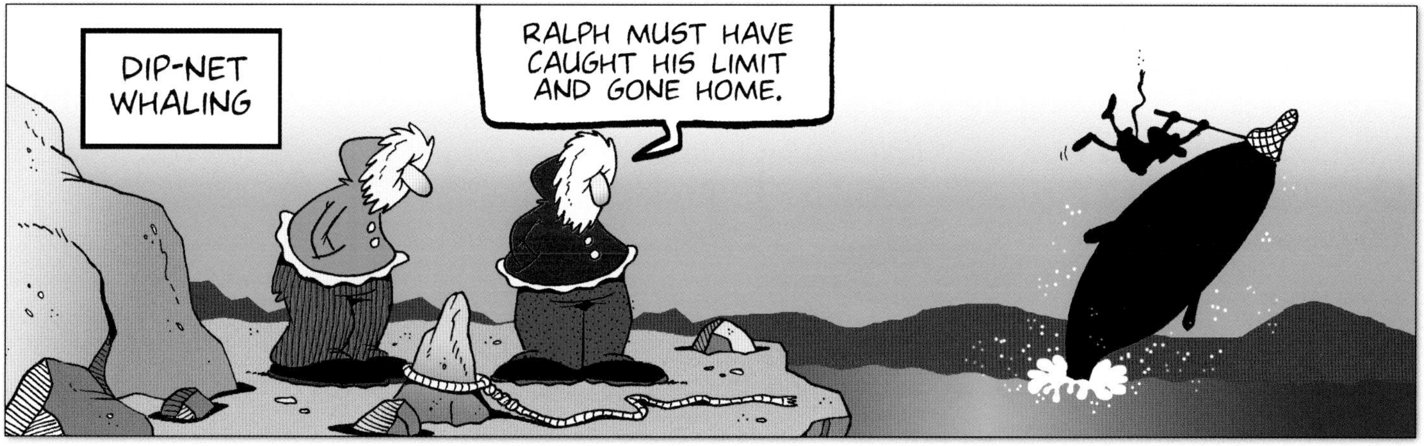
DIP-NET WHALING
RALPH MUST HAVE CAUGHT HIS LIMIT AND GONE HOME.

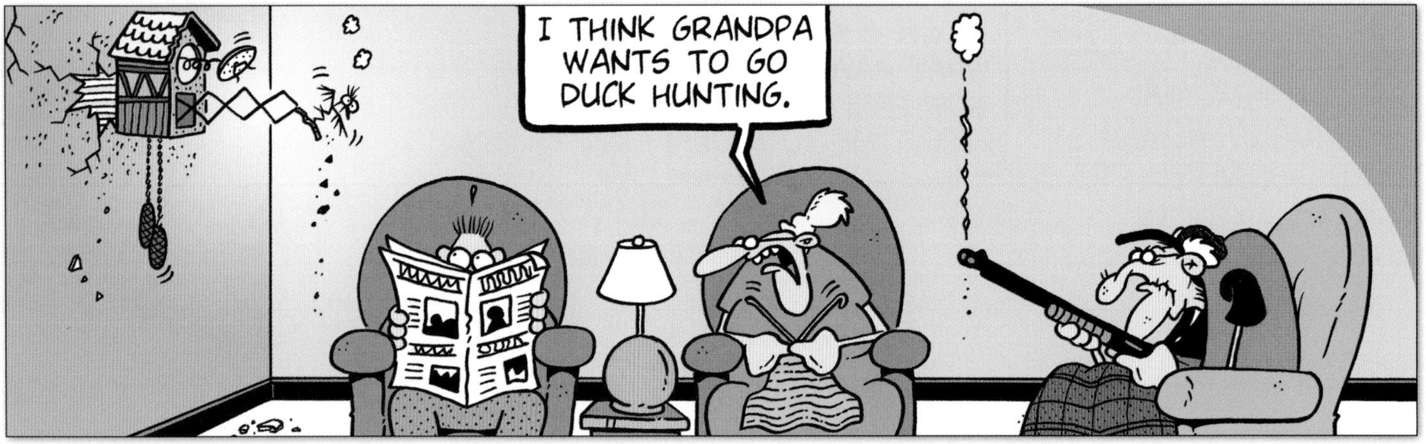
I THINK GRANDPA WANTS TO GO DUCK HUNTING.

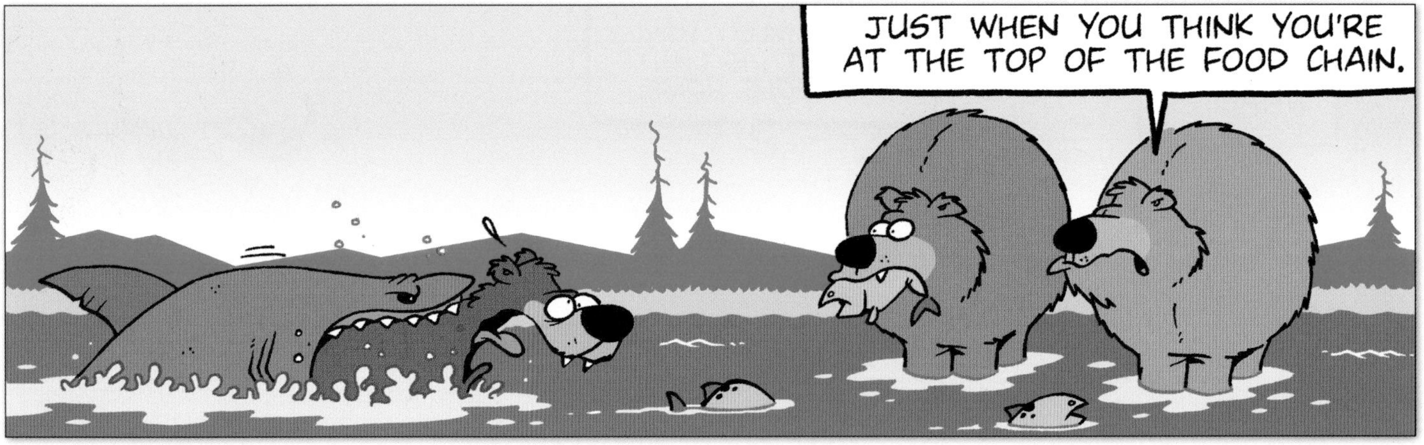
JUST WHEN YOU THINK YOU'RE AT THE TOP OF THE FOOD CHAIN.

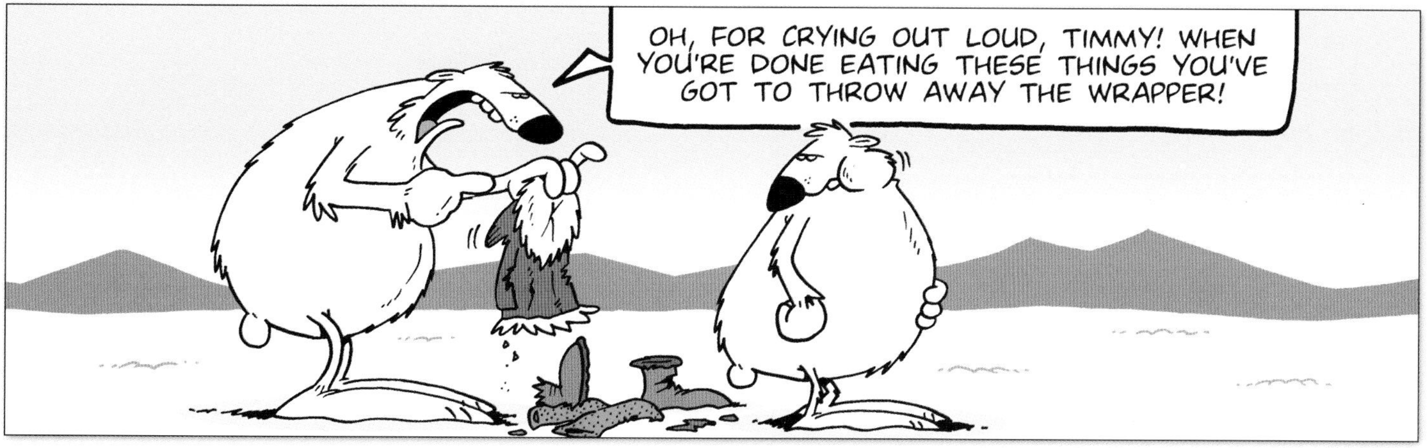
OH, FOR CRYING OUT LOUD, TIMMY! WHEN YOU'RE DONE EATING THESE THINGS YOU'VE GOT TO THROW AWAY THE WRAPPER!

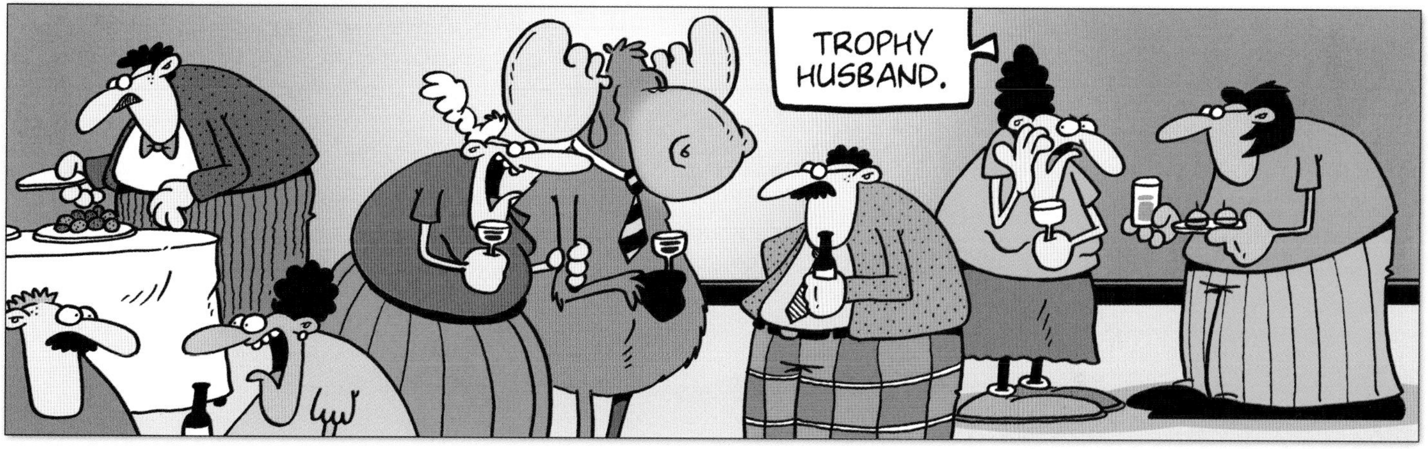
TROPHY HUSBAND.

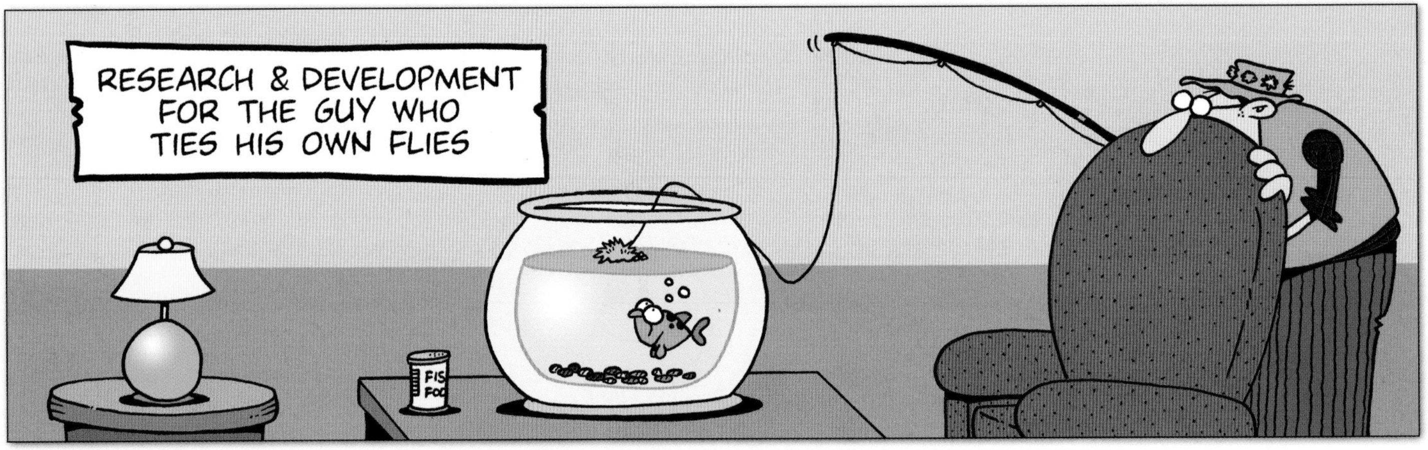
RESEARCH & DEVELOPMENT FOR THE GUY WHO TIES HIS OWN FLIES

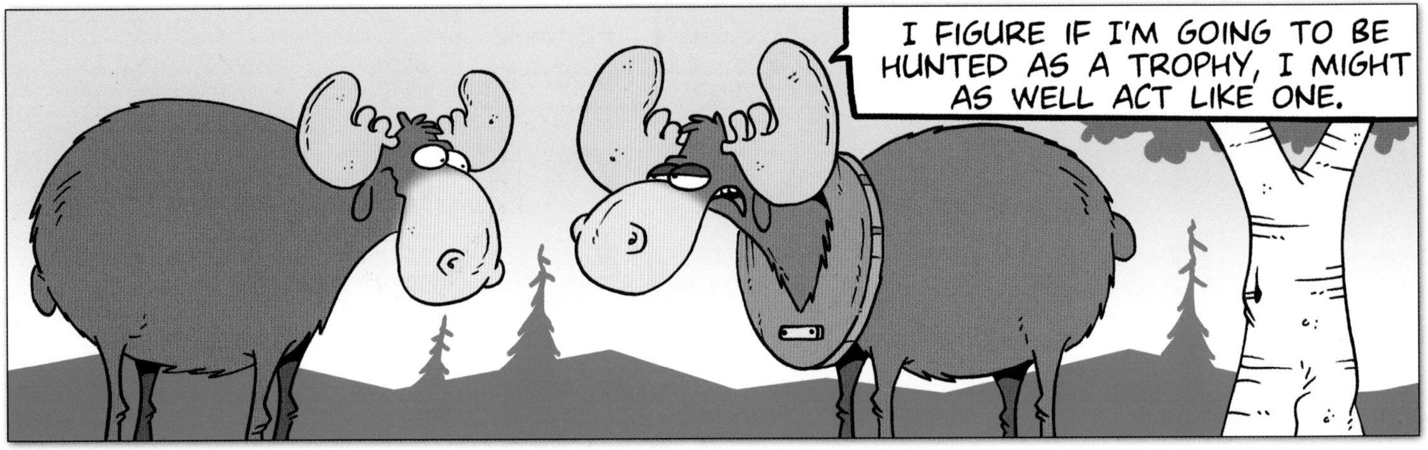
I FIGURE IF I'M GOING TO BE HUNTED AS A TROPHY, I MIGHT AS WELL ACT LIKE ONE.

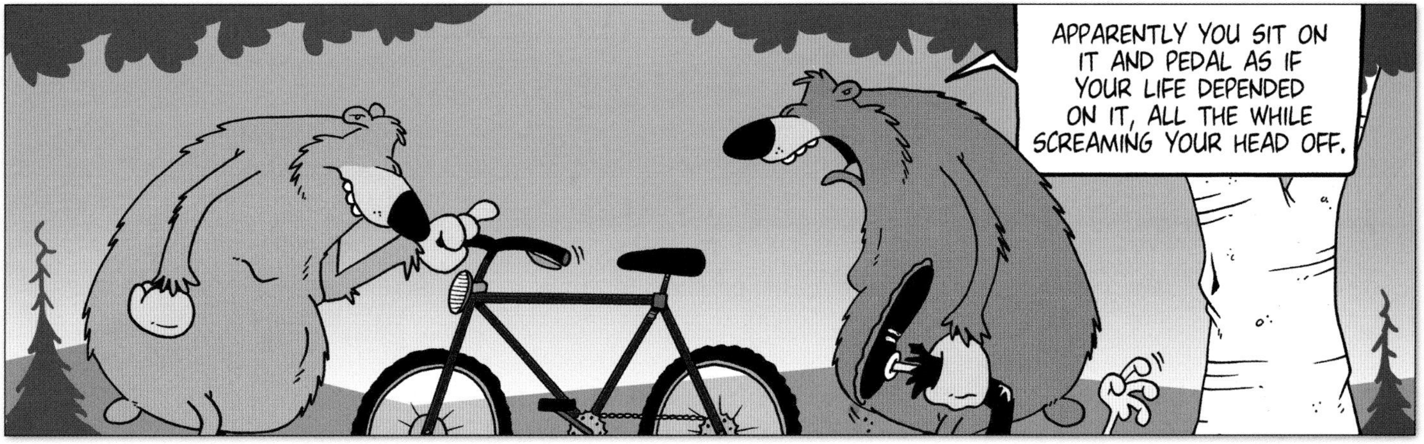
APPARENTLY YOU SIT ON IT AND PEDAL AS IF YOUR LIFE DEPENDED ON IT, ALL THE WHILE SCREAMING YOUR HEAD OFF.

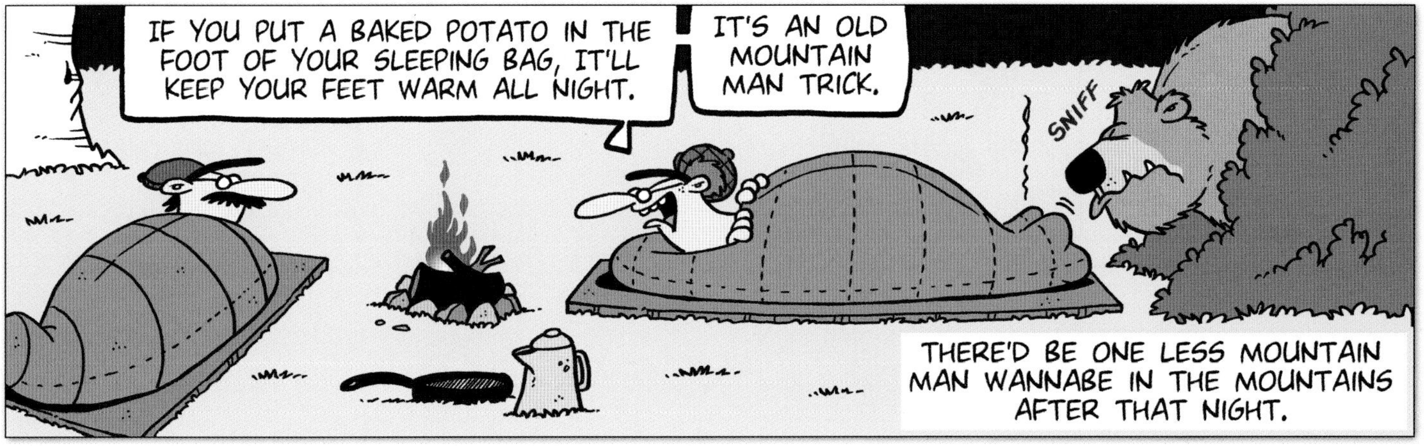
IF YOU PUT A BAKED POTATO IN THE FOOT OF YOUR SLEEPING BAG, IT'LL KEEP YOUR FEET WARM ALL NIGHT.
IT'S AN OLD MOUNTAIN MAN TRICK.
SNIFF
THERE'D BE ONE LESS MOUNTAIN MAN WANNABE IN THE MOUNTAINS AFTER THAT NIGHT.

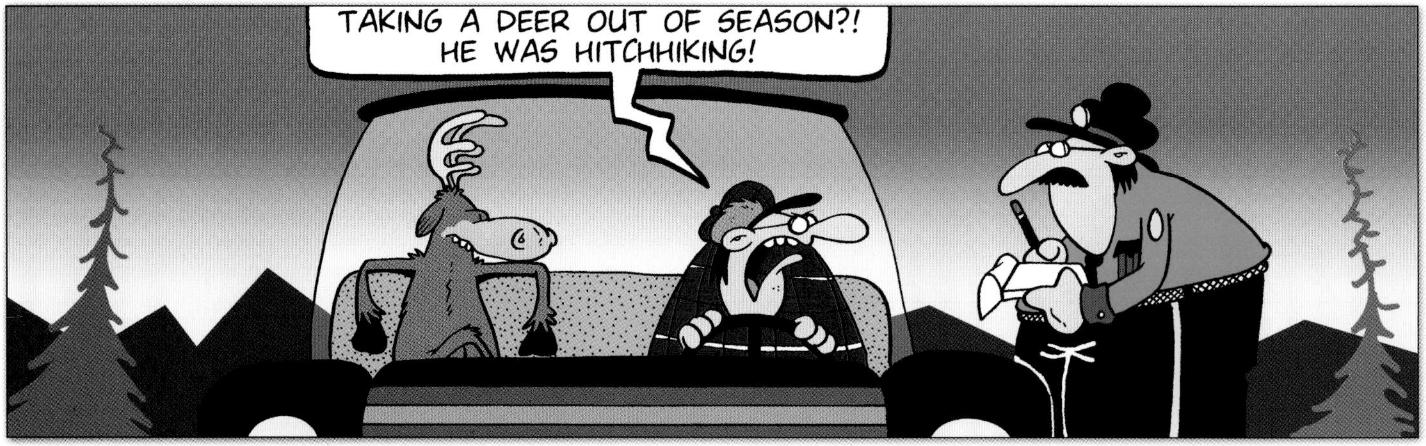
TAKING A DEER OUT OF SEASON?! HE WAS HITCHHIKING!

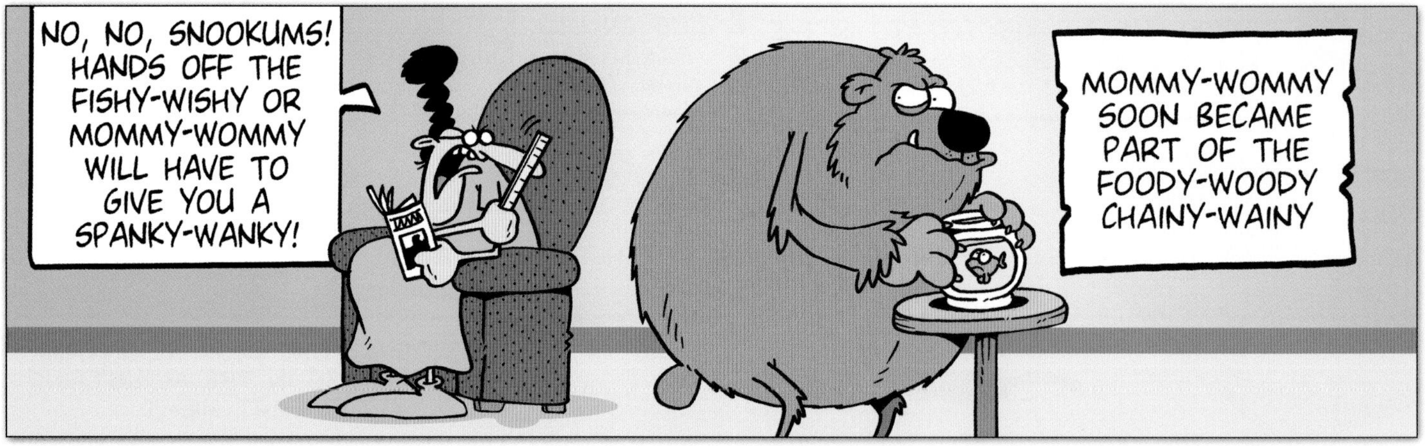
NO, NO, SNOOKUMS! HANDS OFF THE FISHY-WISHY OR MOMMY-WOMMY WILL HAVE TO GIVE YOU A SPANKY-WANKY!
MOMMY-WOMMY SOON BECAME PART OF THE FOODY-WOODY CHAINY-WAINY

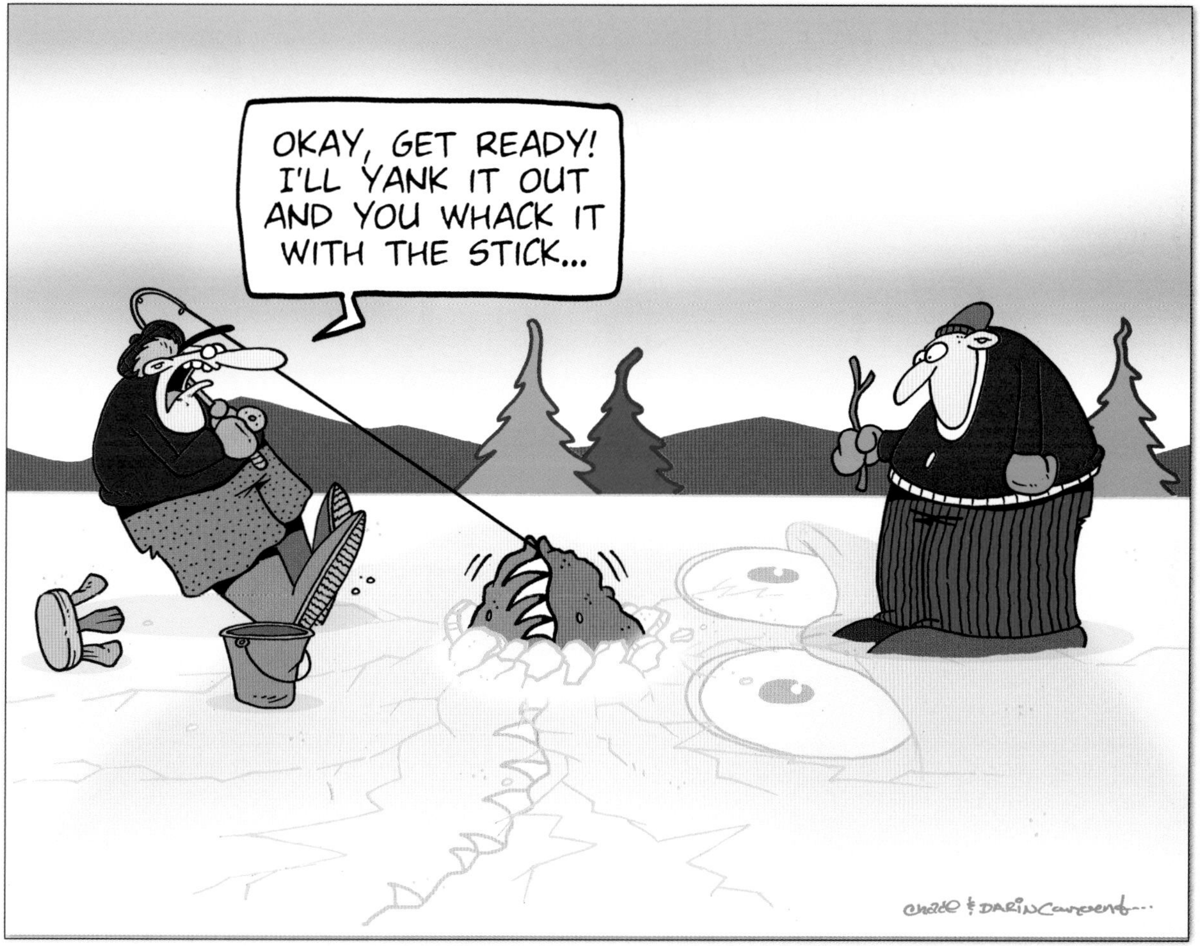
OKAY, GET READY! I'LL YANK IT OUT AND YOU WHACK IT WITH THE STICK...
Chade & DARIN Carpenter...

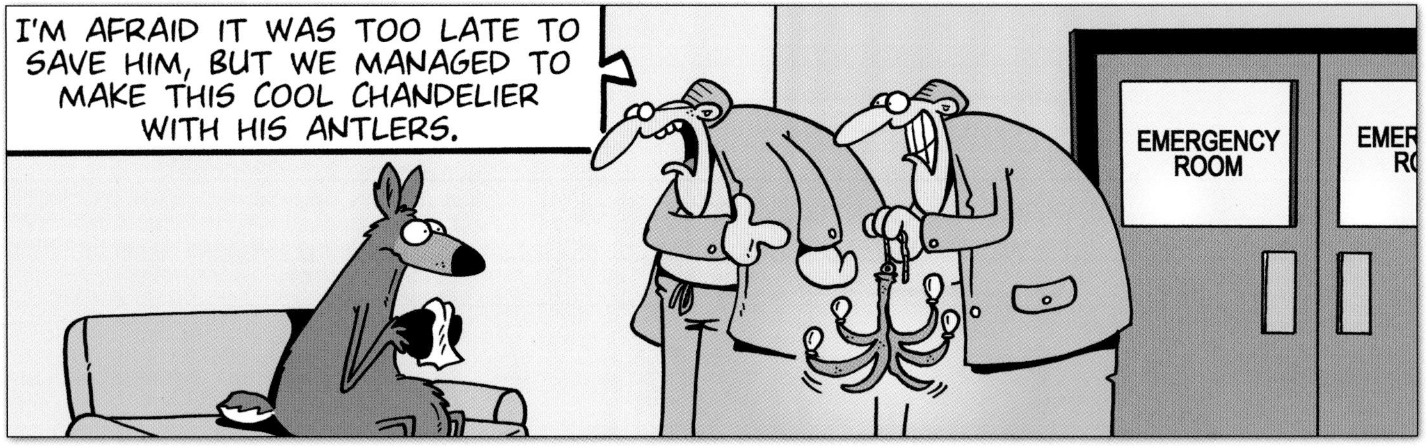
I'M AFRAID IT WAS TOO LATE TO SAVE HIM, BUT WE MANAGED TO MAKE THIS COOL CHANDELIER WITH HIS ANTLERS.
EMERGENCY ROOM

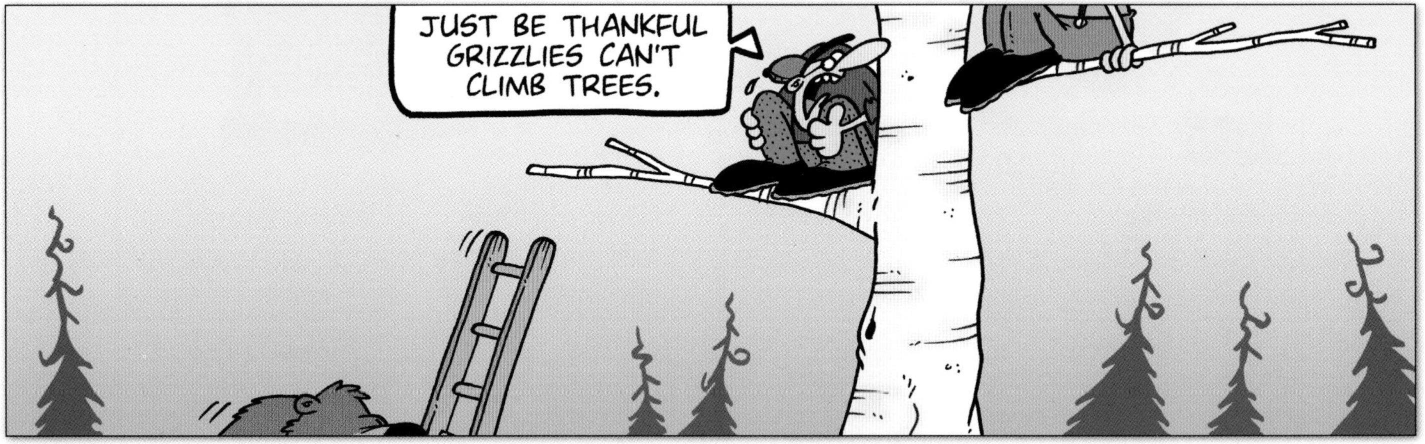
JUST BE THANKFUL GRIZZLIES CAN'T CLIMB TREES.

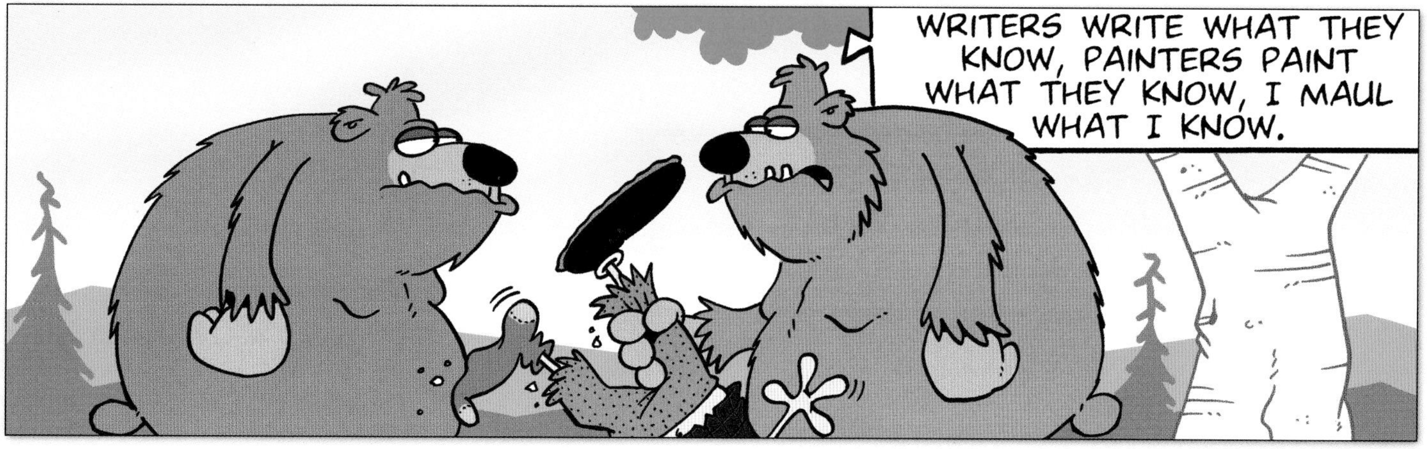
WRITERS WRITE WHAT THEY KNOW, PAINTERS PAINT WHAT THEY KNOW, I MAUL WHAT I KNOW.

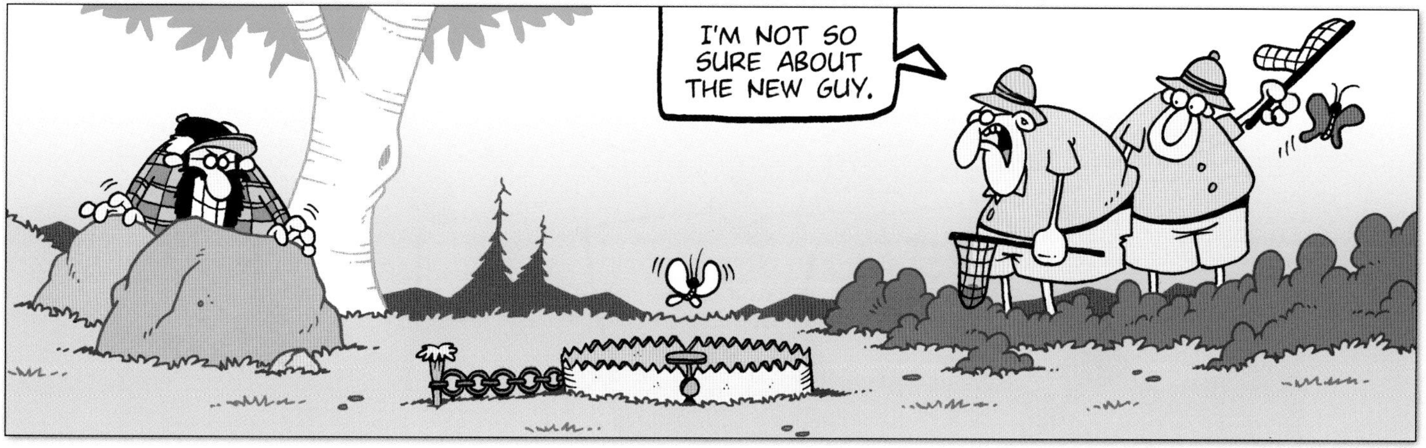
I'M NOT SO SURE ABOUT THE NEW GUY.

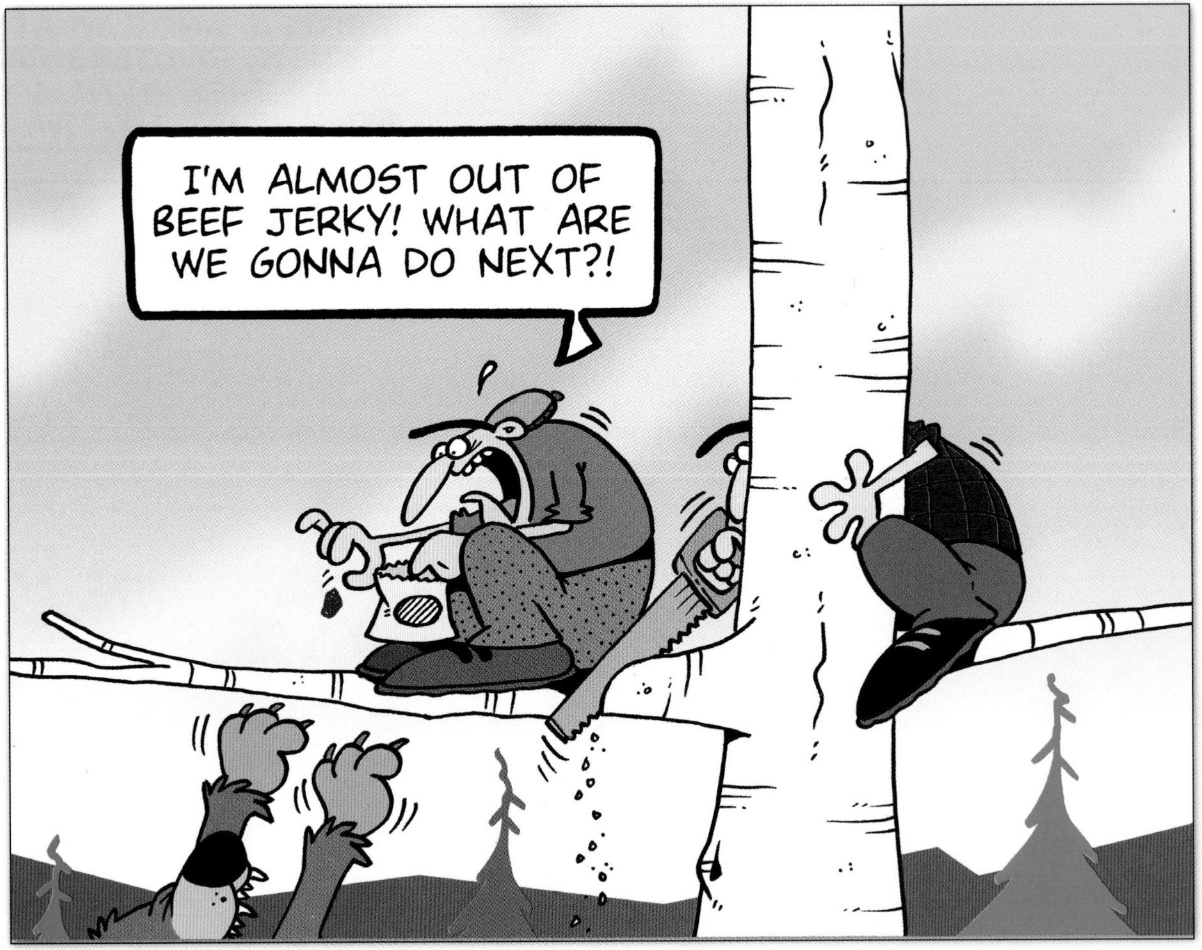
I'M ALMOST OUT OF BEEF JERKY! WHAT ARE WE GONNA DO NEXT?!

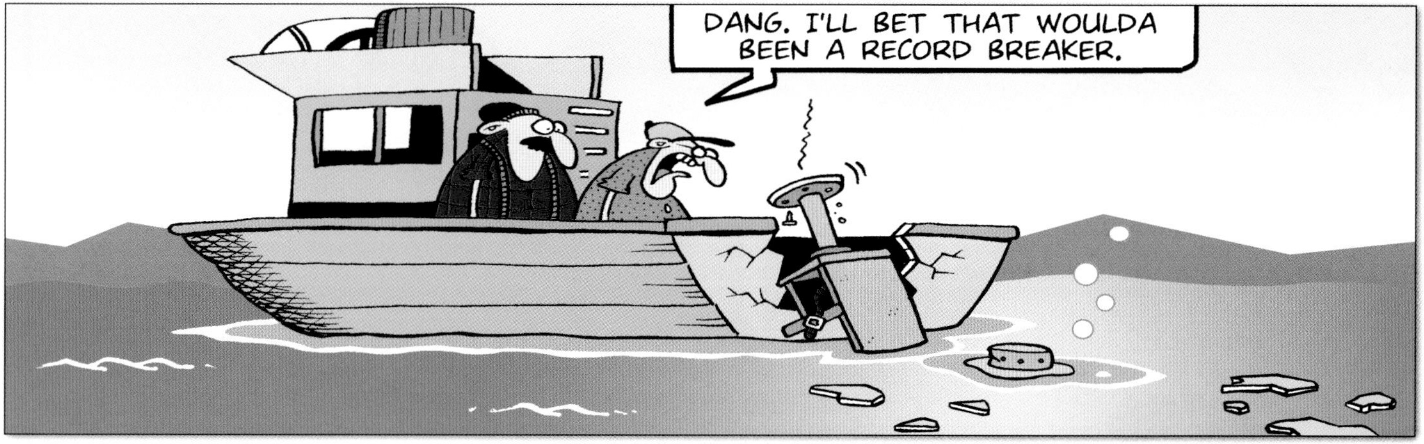
DANG. I'LL BET THAT WOULDA BEEN A RECORD BREAKER.

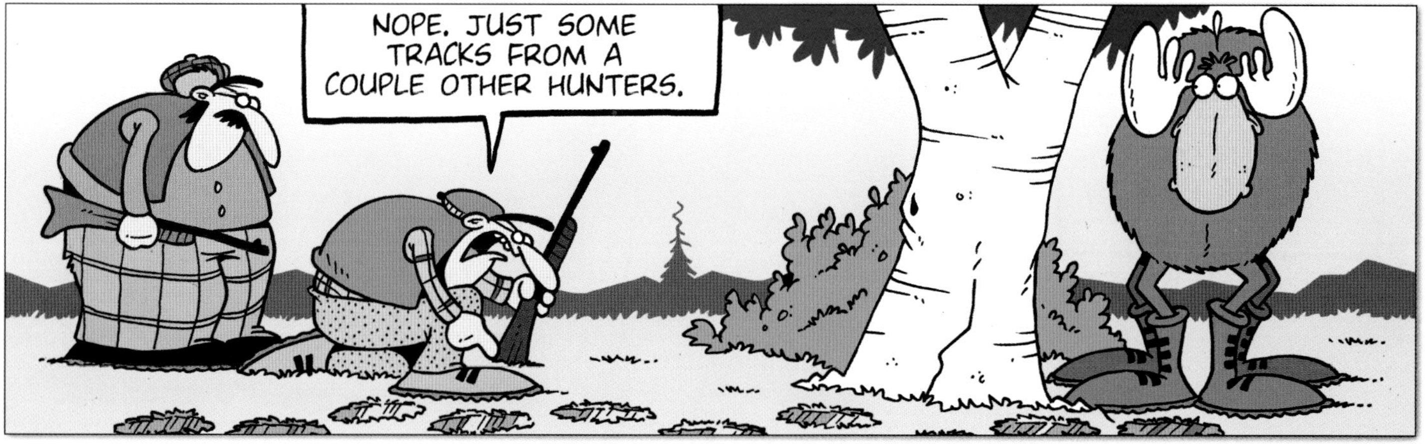
NOPE. JUST SOME TRACKS FROM A COUPLE OTHER HUNTERS.

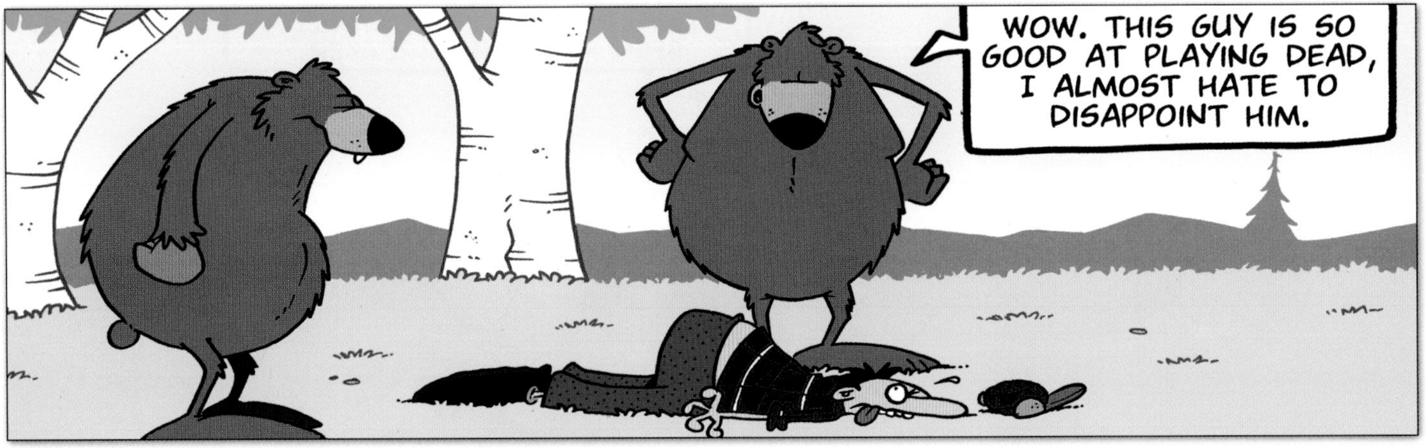
WOW. THIS GUY IS SO GOOD AT PLAYING DEAD, I ALMOST HATE TO DISAPPOINT HIM.

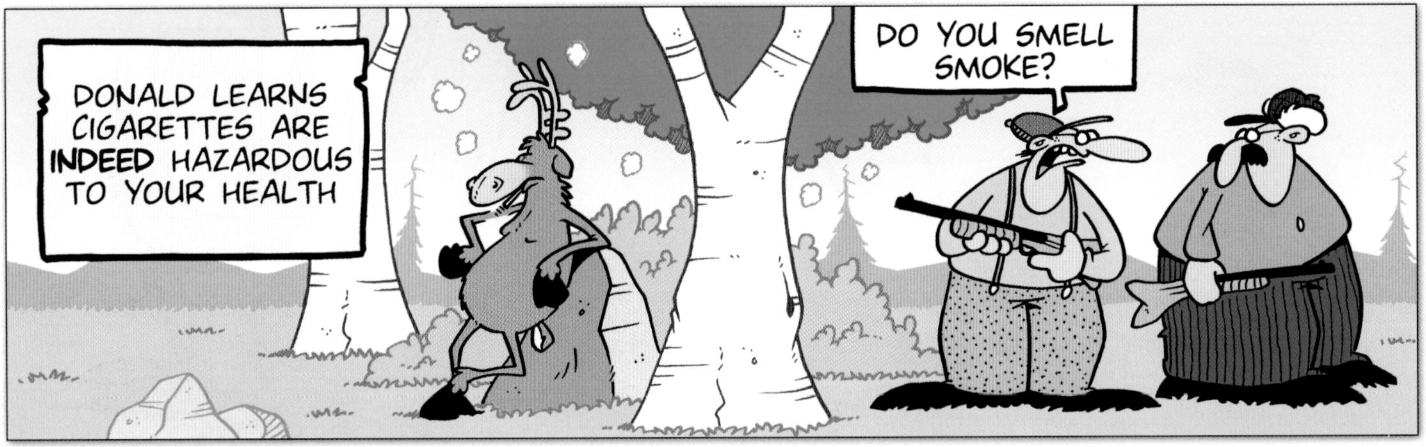
DONALD LEARNS CIGARETTES ARE **INDEED** HAZARDOUS TO YOUR HEALTH
DO YOU SMELL SMOKE?

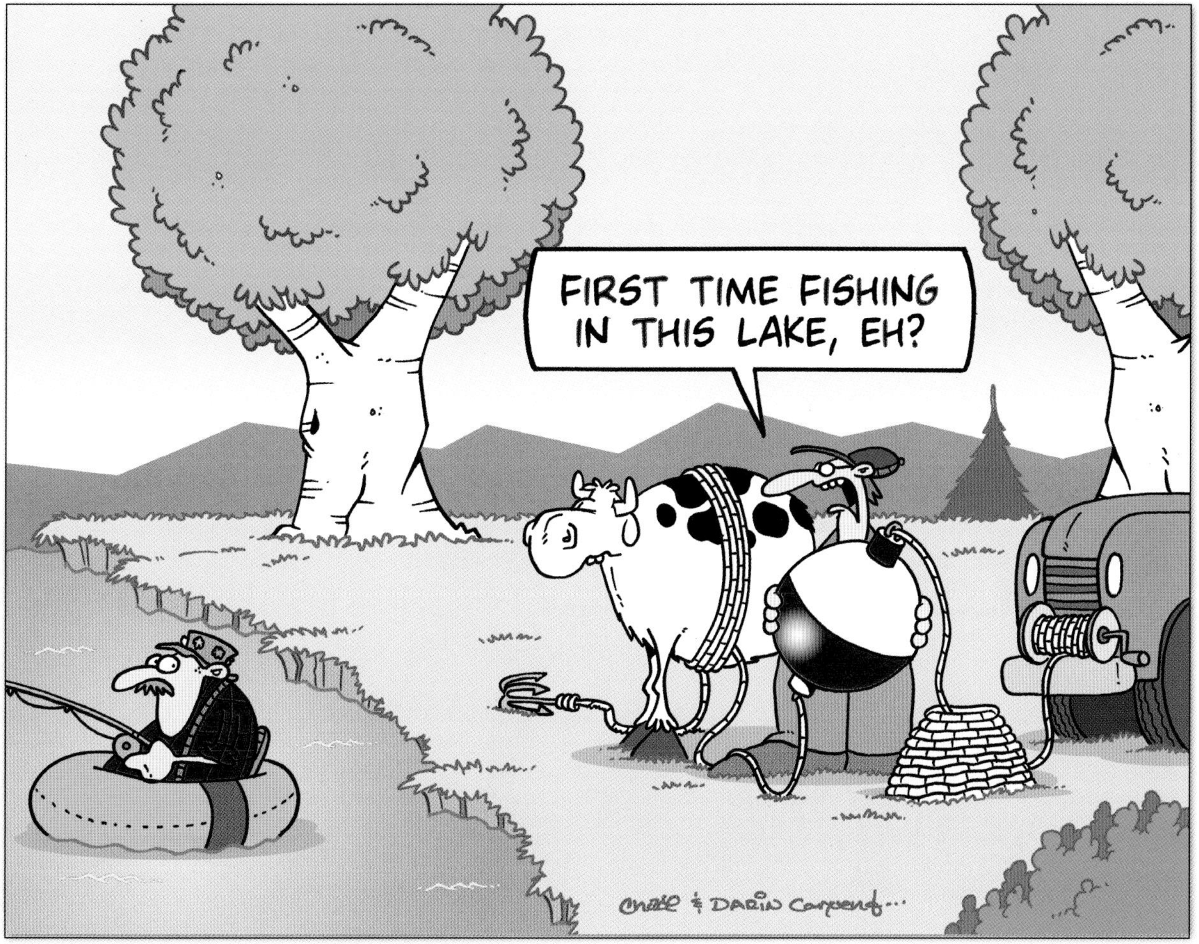
FIRST TIME FISHING IN THIS LAKE, EH?
CHAD & DARIN CARPENTER...

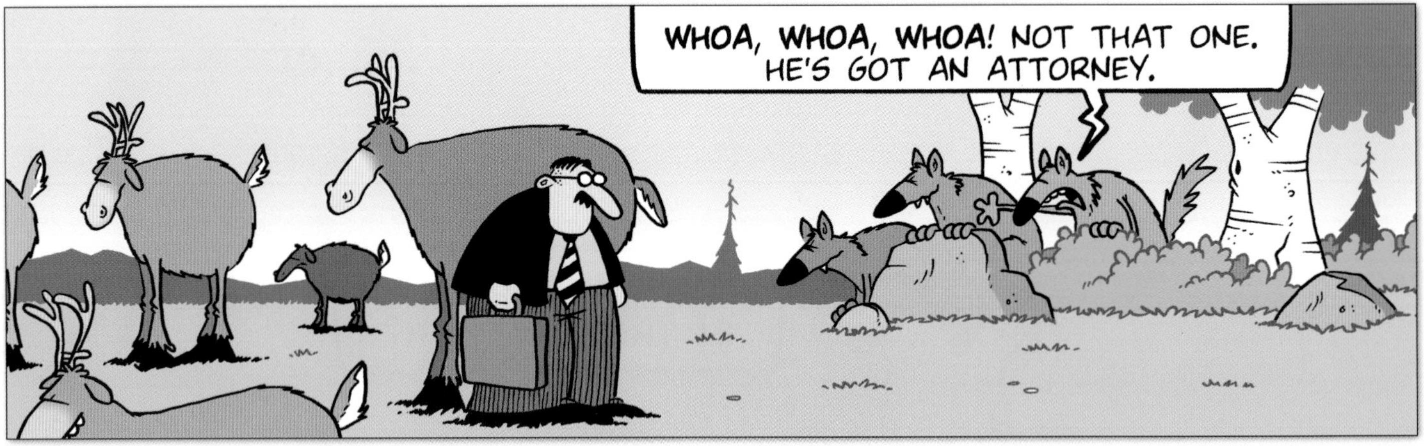
WHOA, WHOA, WHOA! NOT THAT ONE. HE'S GOT AN ATTORNEY.

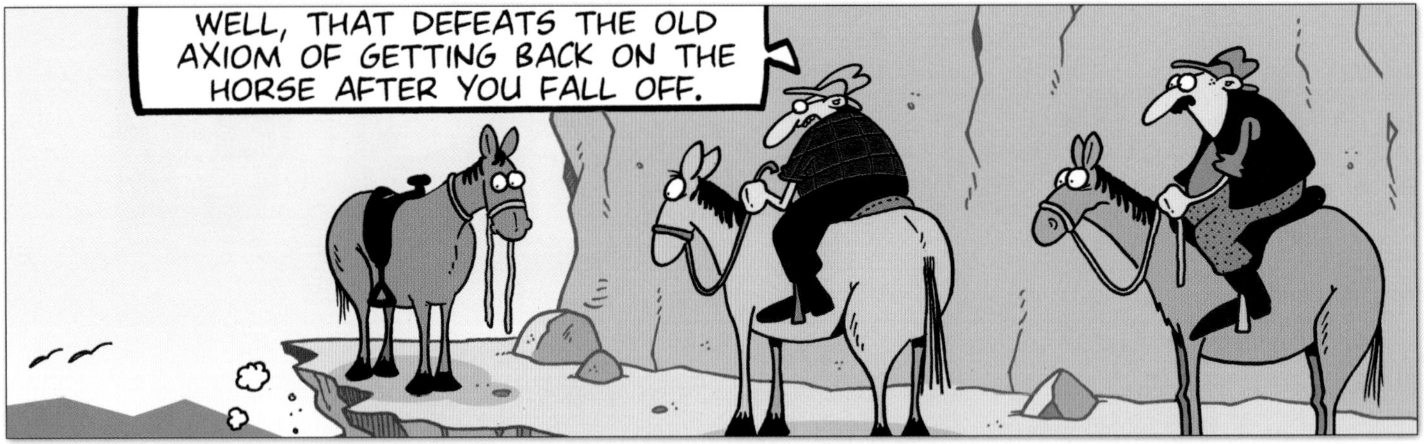
WELL, THAT DEFEATS THE OLD AXIOM OF GETTING BACK ON THE HORSE AFTER YOU FALL OFF.

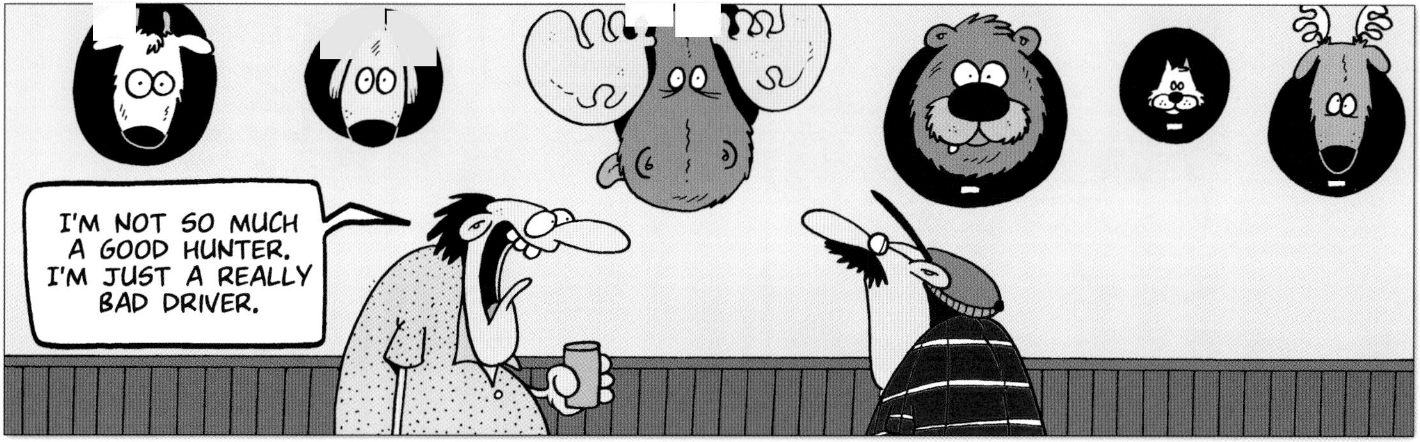
I'M NOT SO MUCH A GOOD HUNTER. I'M JUST A REALLY BAD DRIVER.

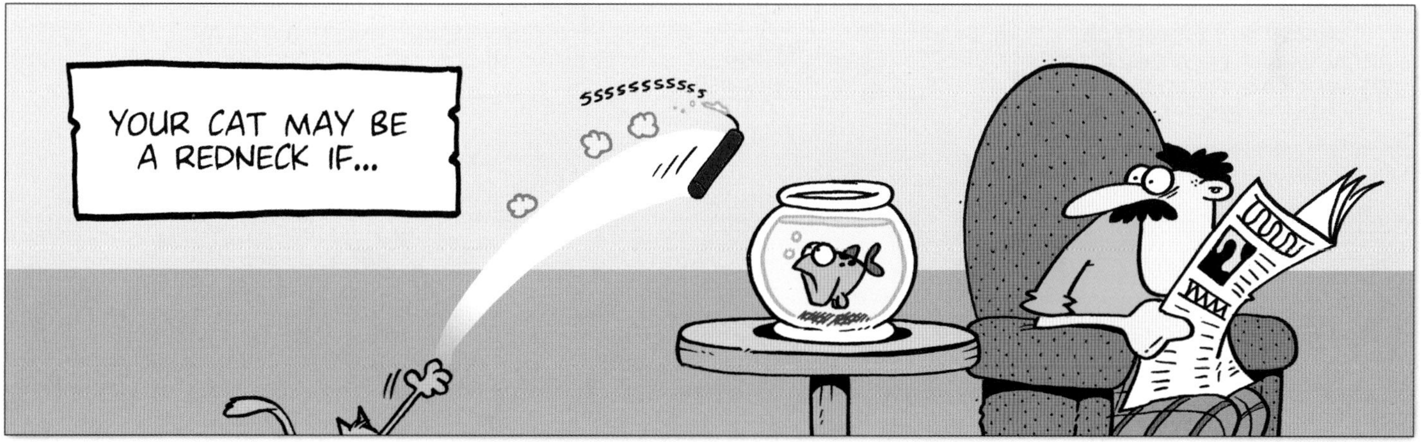
YOUR CAT MAY BE A REDNECK IF...
SSSSSSSSSSSS

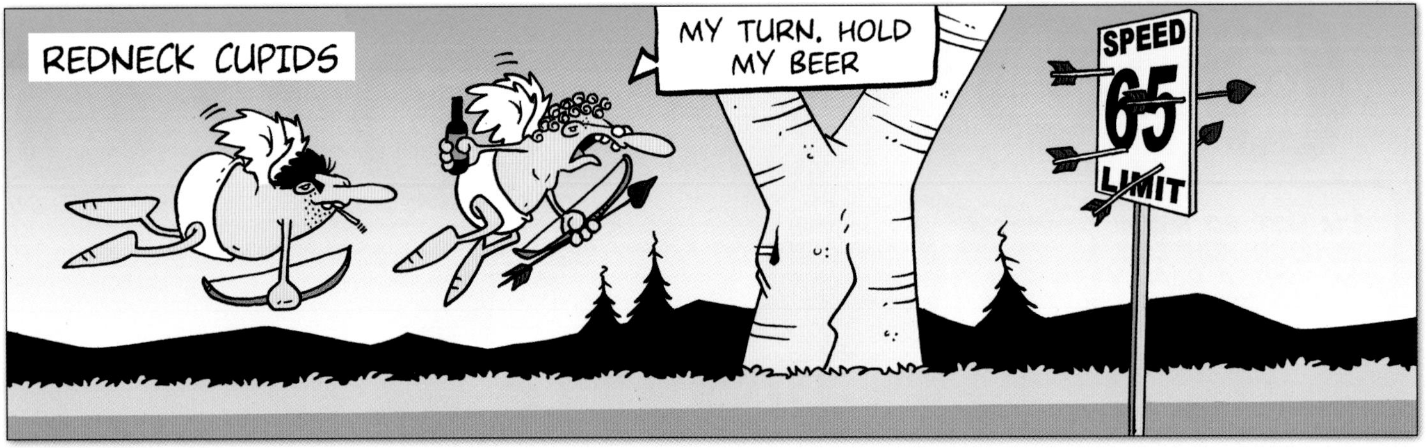
REDNECK CUPIDS
MY TURN. HOLD MY BEER
SPEED 65 LIMIT

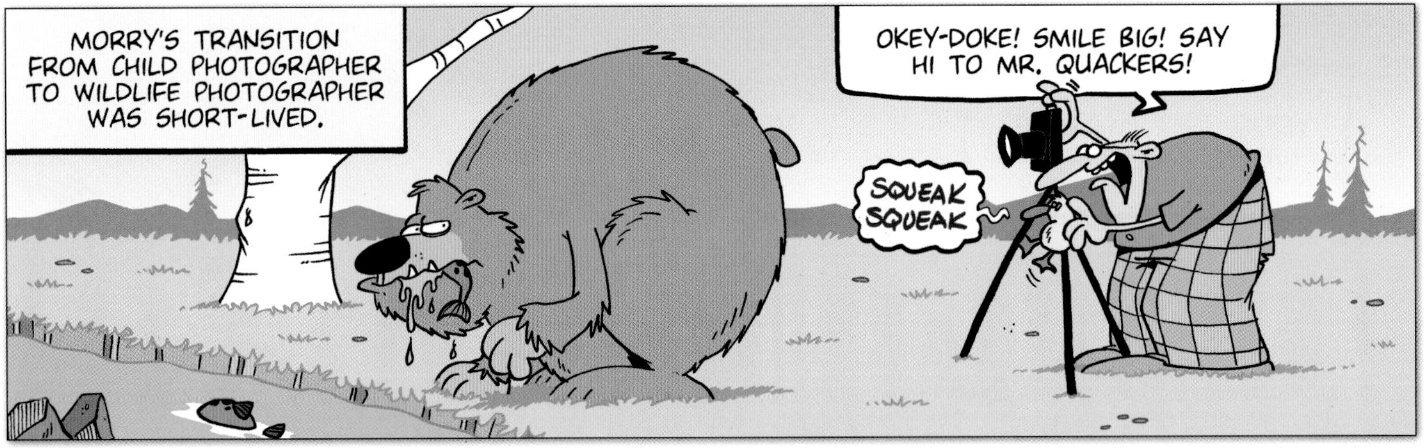
MORRY'S TRANSITION FROM CHILD PHOTOGRAPHER TO WILDLIFE PHOTOGRAPHER WAS SHORT-LIVED.
OKEY-DOKE! SMILE BIG! SAY HI TO MR. QUACKERS!
SQUEAK SQUEAK

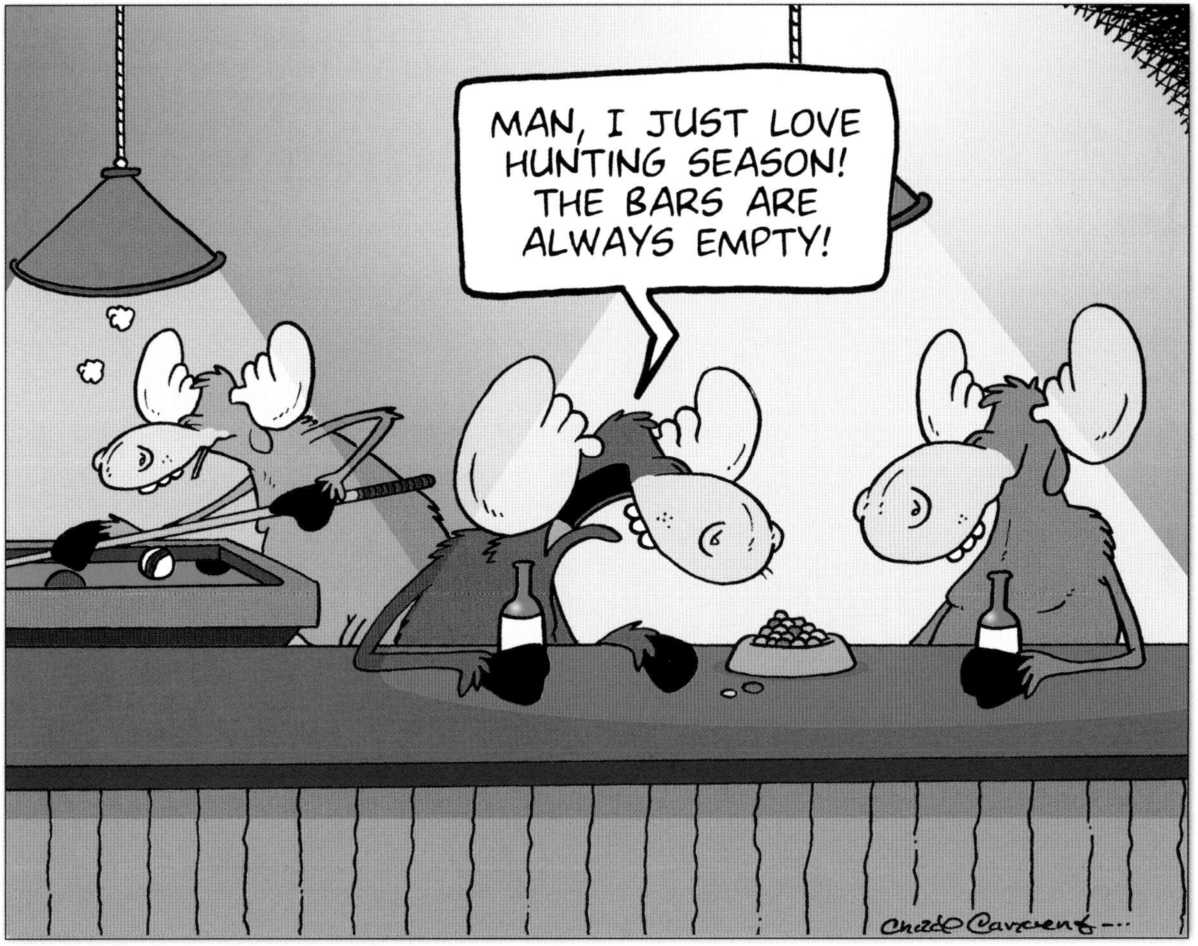
MAN, I JUST LOVE HUNTING SEASON! THE BARS ARE ALWAYS EMPTY!

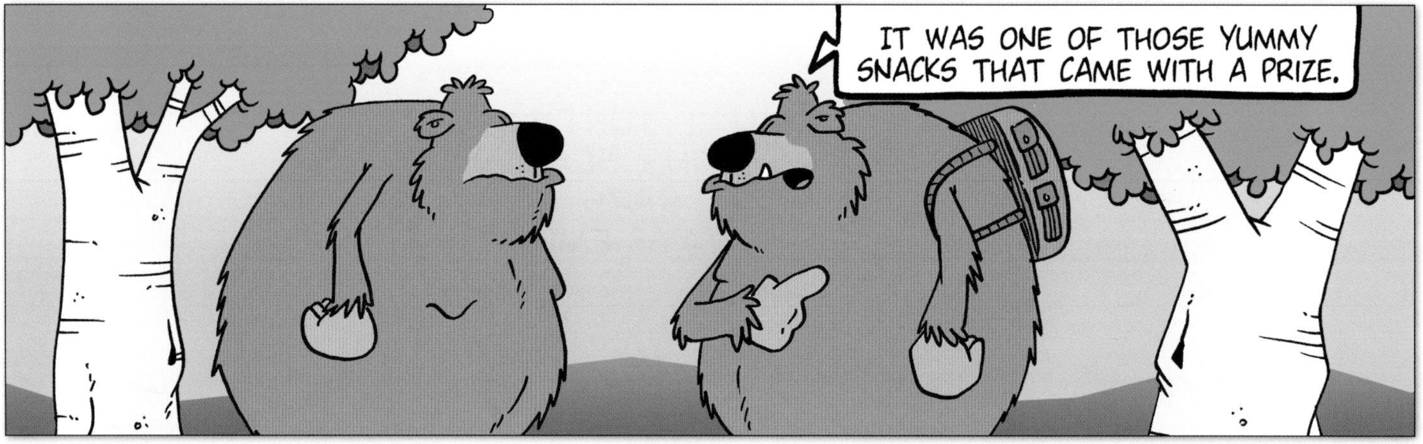
IT WAS ONE OF THOSE YUMMY SNACKS THAT CAME WITH A PRIZE.

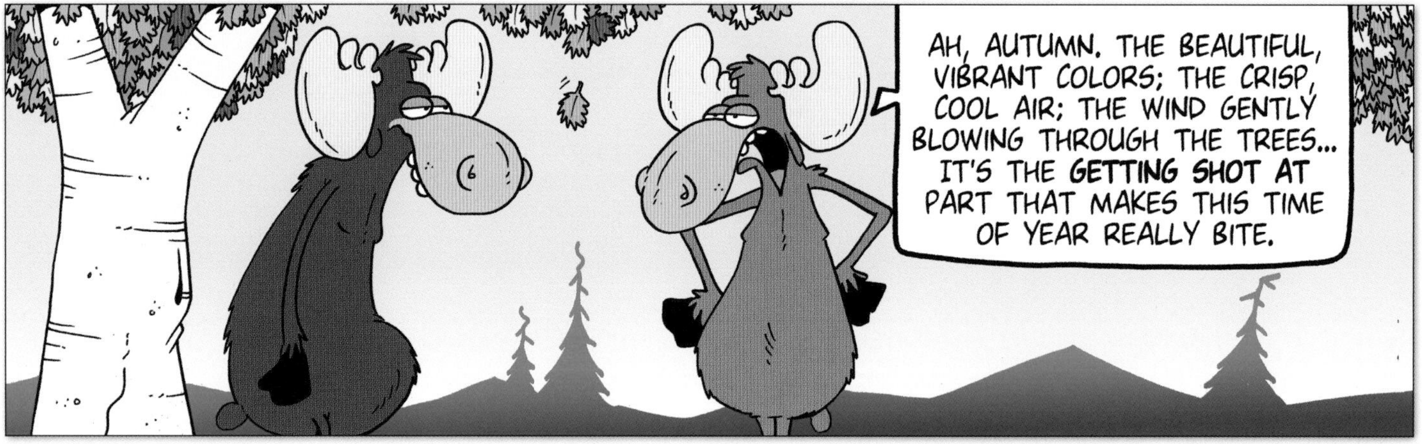
AH, AUTUMN. THE BEAUTIFUL, VIBRANT COLORS; THE CRISP, COOL AIR; THE WIND GENTLY BLOWING THROUGH THE TREES... IT'S THE **GETTING SHOT AT** PART THAT MAKES THIS TIME OF YEAR REALLY BITE.

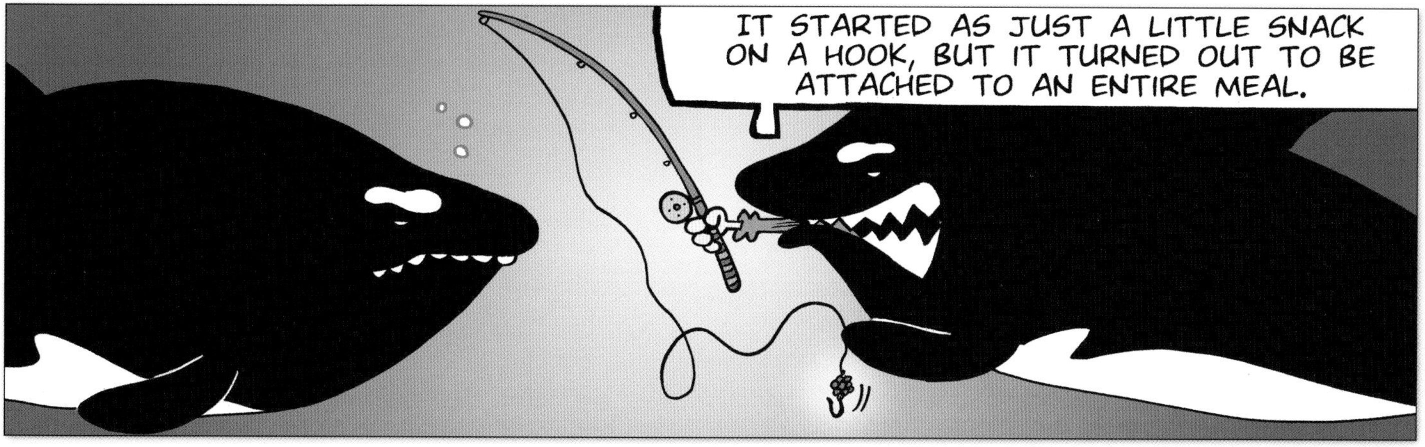
IT STARTED AS JUST A LITTLE SNACK ON A HOOK, BUT IT TURNED OUT TO BE ATTACHED TO AN ENTIRE MEAL.

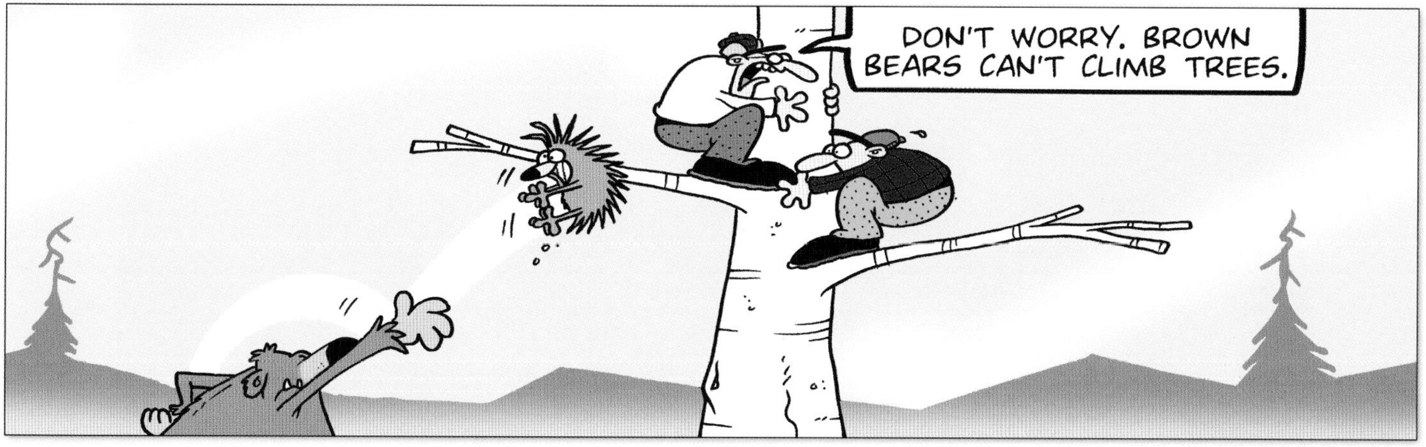
DON'T WORRY. BROWN BEARS CAN'T CLIMB TREES.

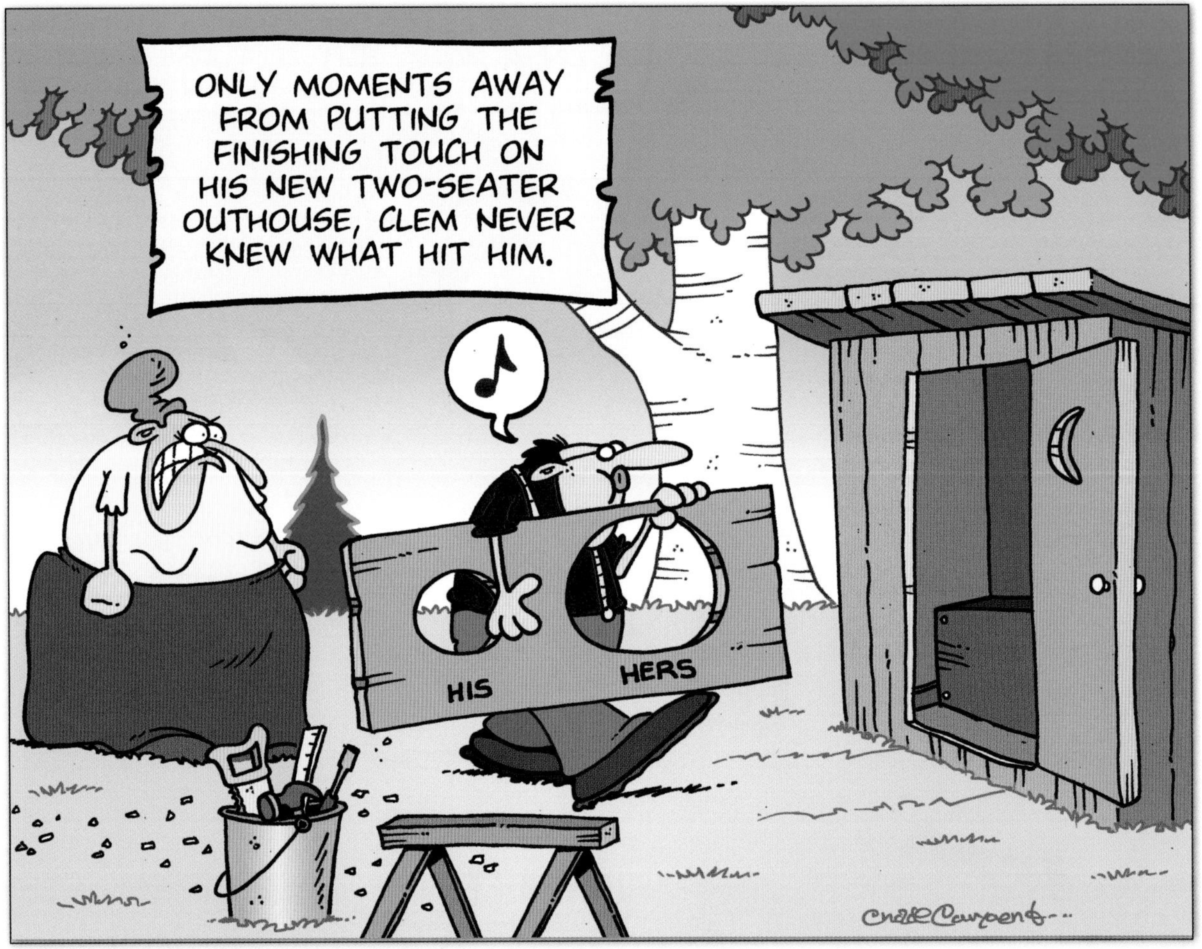
ONLY MOMENTS AWAY FROM PUTTING THE FINISHING TOUCH ON HIS NEW TWO-SEATER OUTHOUSE, CLEM NEVER KNEW WHAT HIT HIM.
HIS
HERS

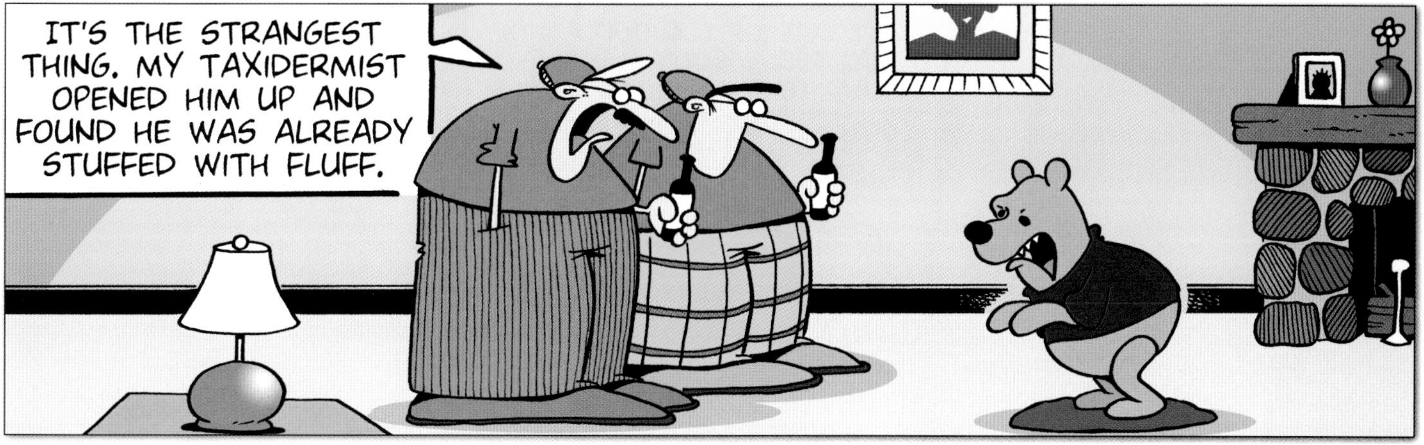
IT'S THE STRANGEST THING. MY TAXIDERMIST OPENED HIM UP AND FOUND HE WAS ALREADY STUFFED WITH FLUFF.

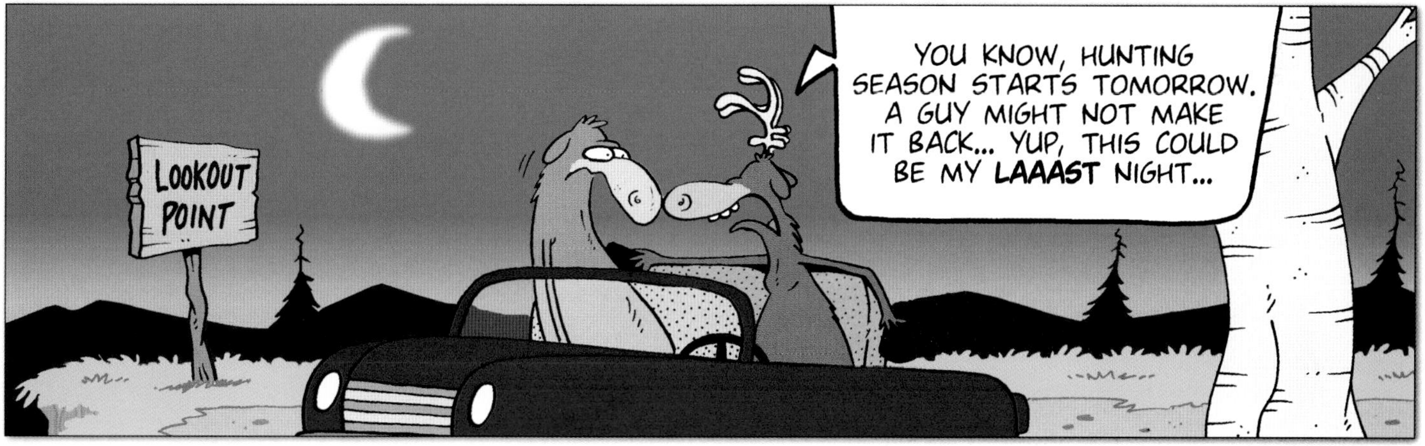
YOU KNOW, HUNTING SEASON STARTS TOMORROW. A GUY MIGHT NOT MAKE IT BACK... YUP, THIS COULD BE MY **LAAAST** NIGHT...
LOOKOUT POINT

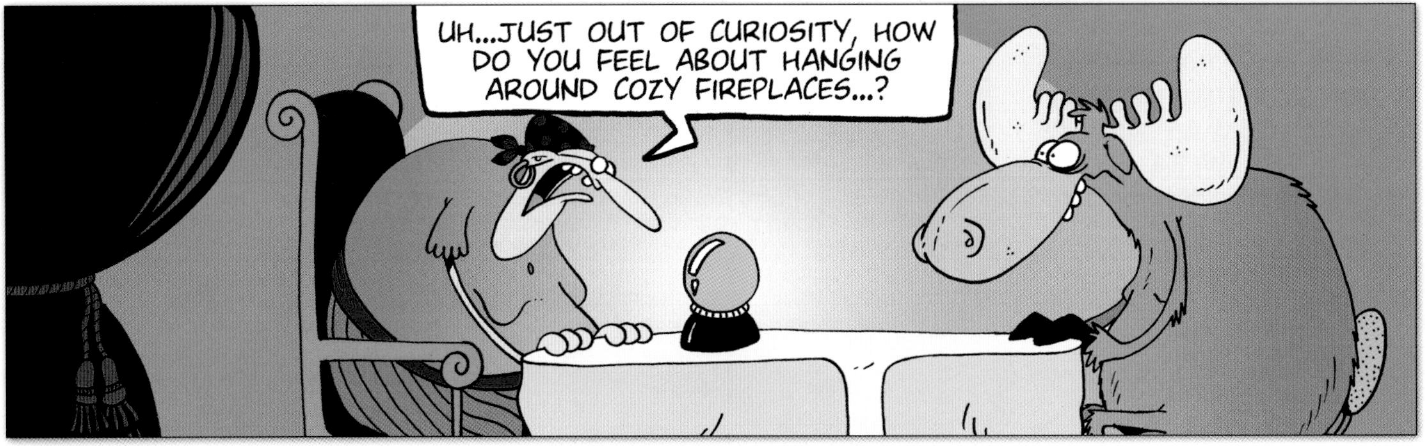
UH...JUST OUT OF CURIOSITY, HOW DO YOU FEEL ABOUT HANGING AROUND COZY FIREPLACES...?

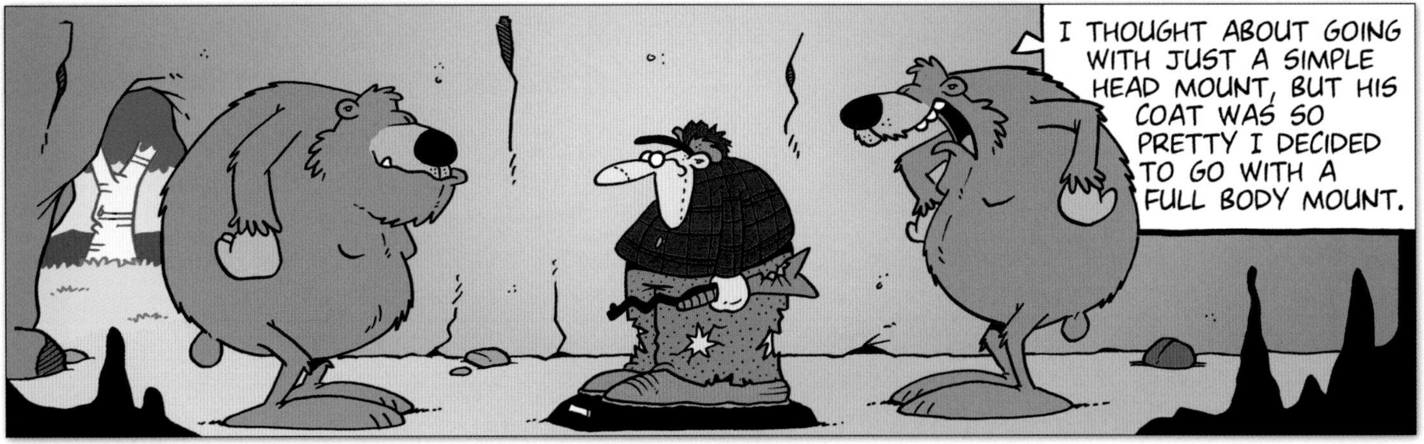
I THOUGHT ABOUT GOING WITH JUST A SIMPLE HEAD MOUNT, BUT HIS COAT WAS SO PRETTY I DECIDED TO GO WITH A FULL BODY MOUNT.

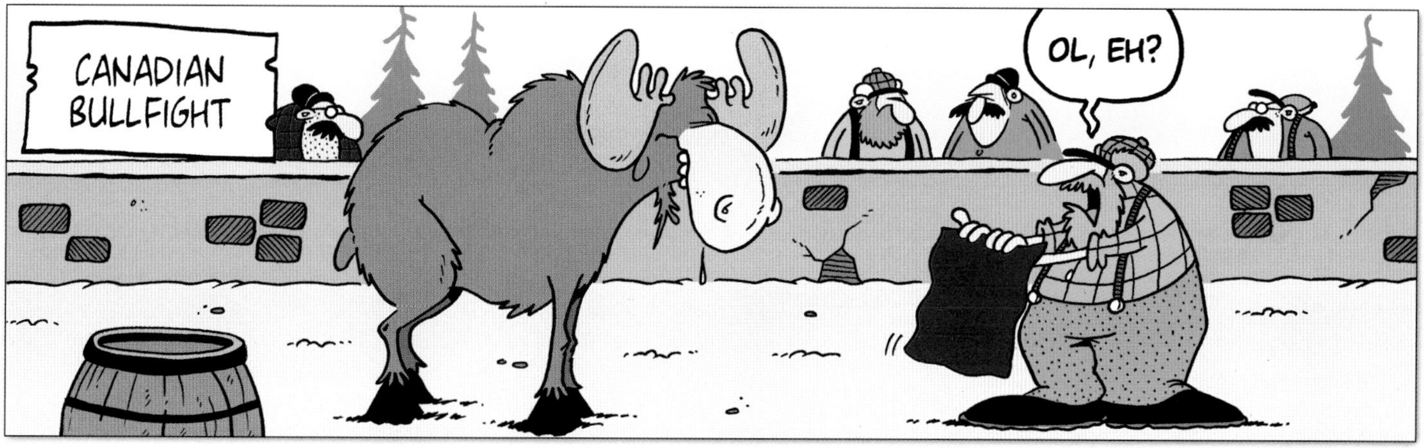
CANADIAN BULLFIGHT
OL, EH?

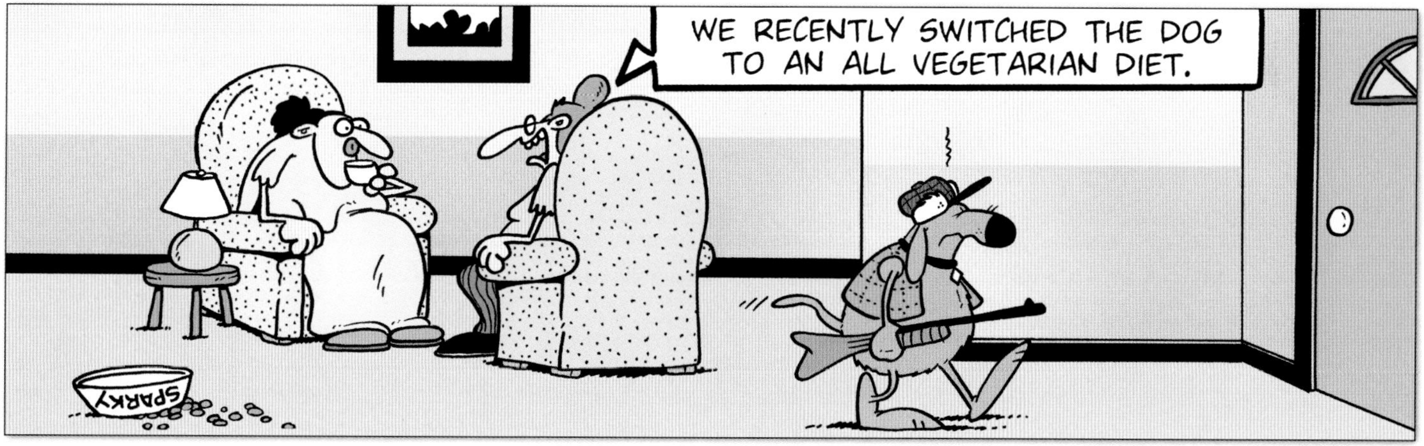
WE RECENTLY SWITCHED THE DOG TO AN ALL VEGETARIAN DIET.
SPARKY

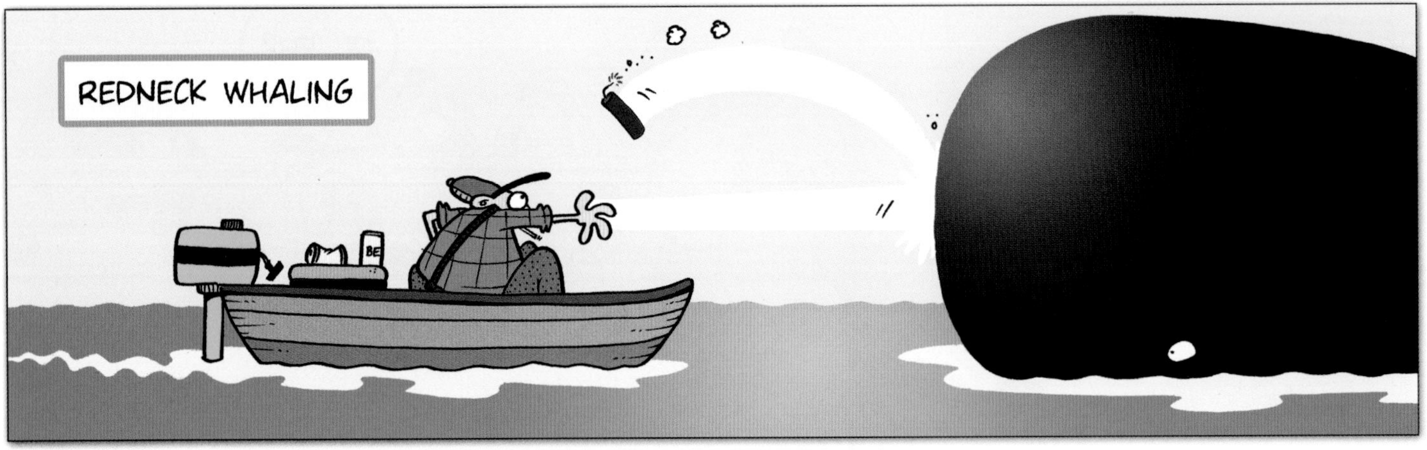
REDNECK WHALING

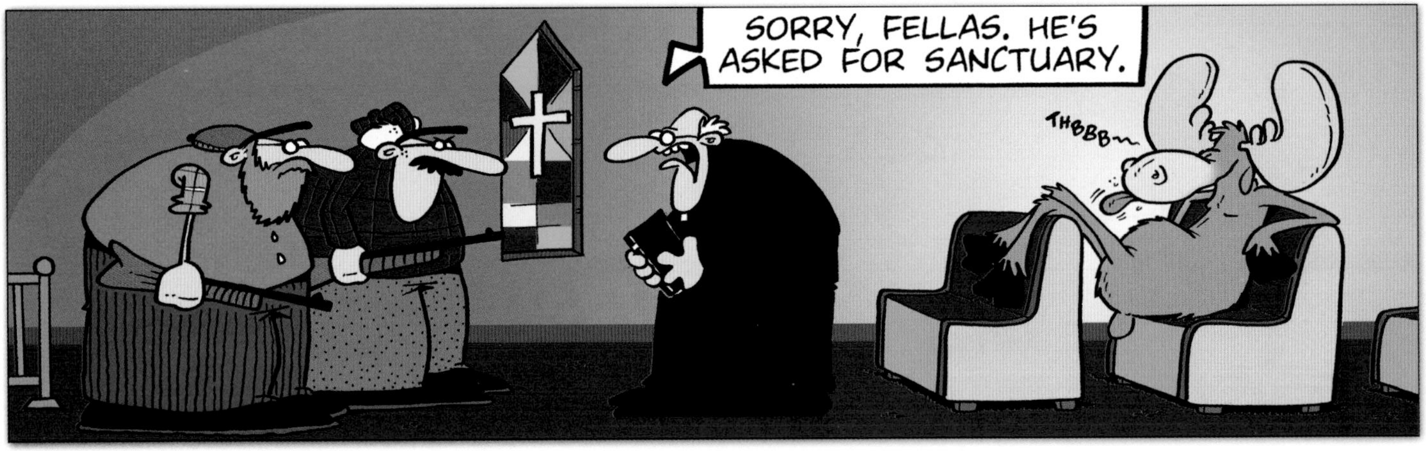
SORRY, FELLAS. HE'S ASKED FOR SANCTUARY.
THBBB

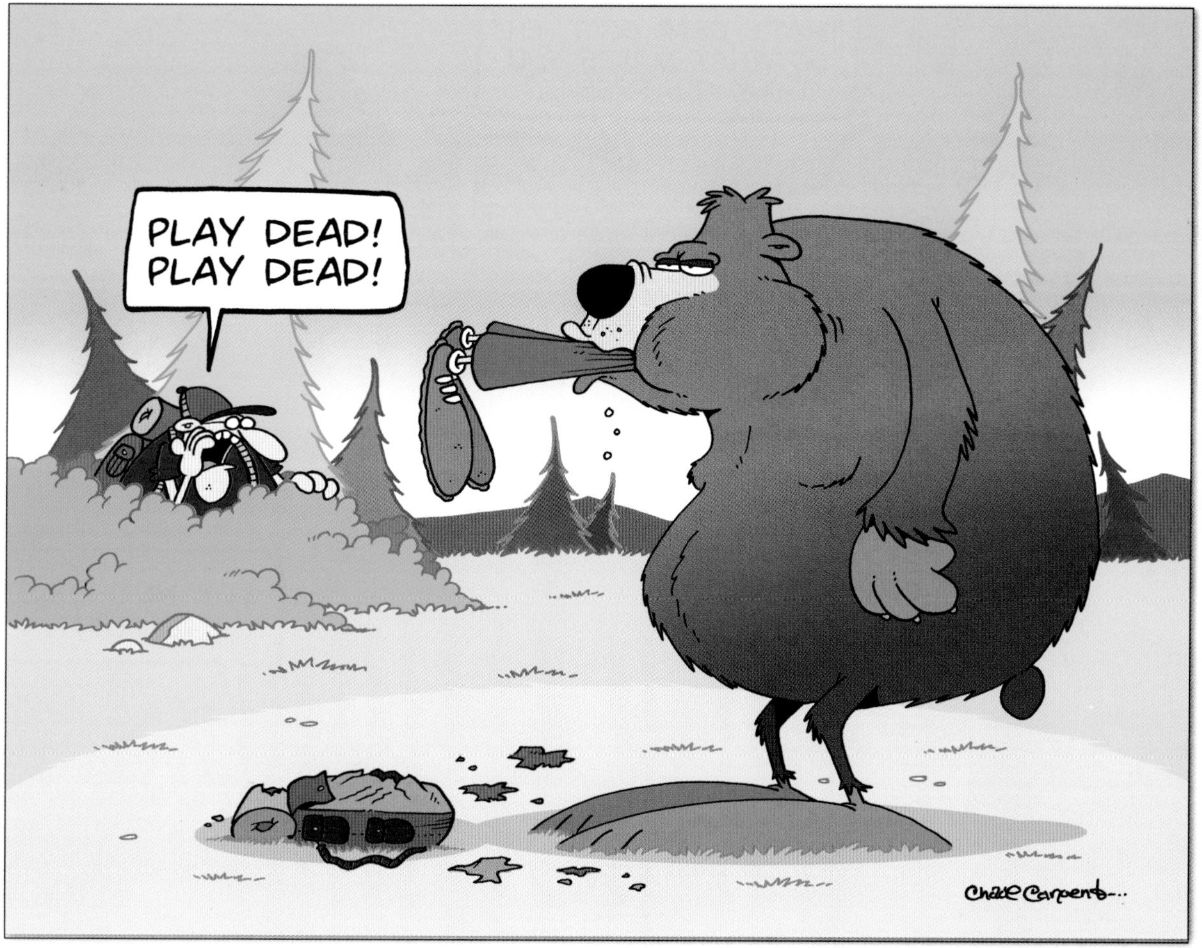
PLAY DEAD!
PLAY DEAD!
Chad Carpenter

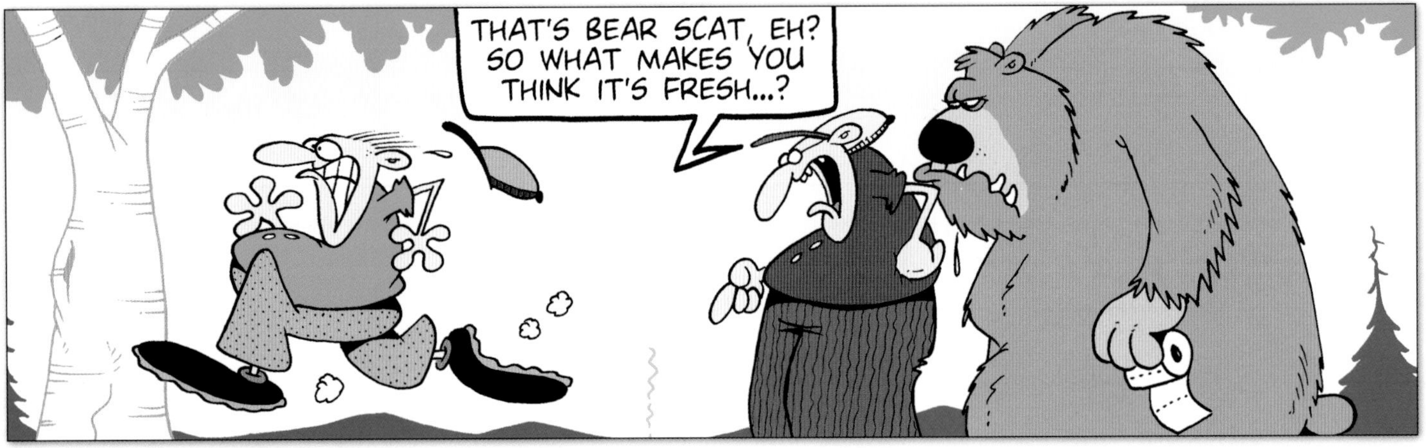
THAT'S BEAR SCAT, EH? SO WHAT MAKES YOU THINK IT'S FRESH...?

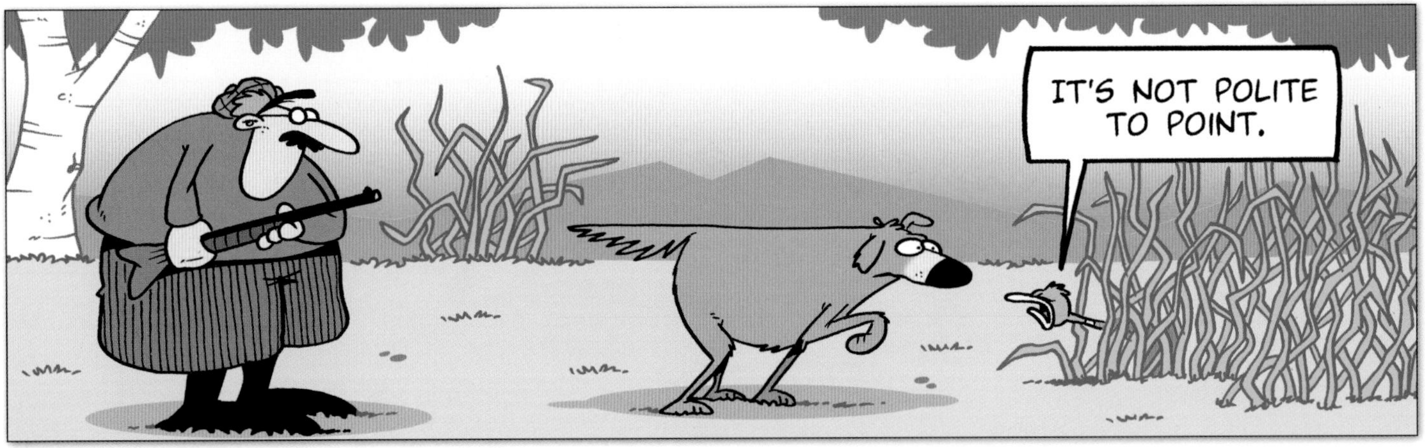
IT'S NOT POLITE TO POINT.

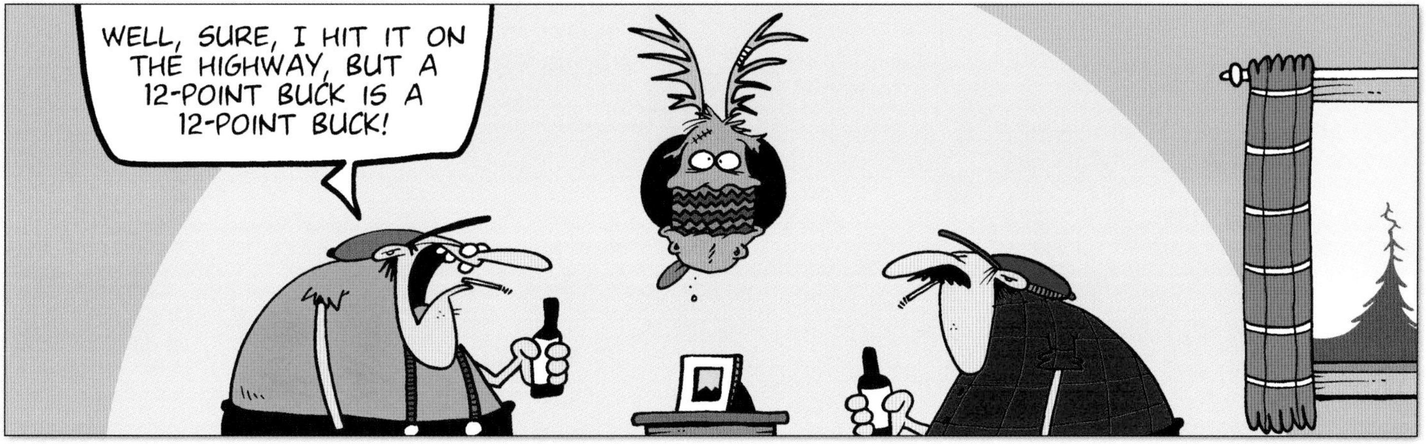
WELL, SURE, I HIT IT ON THE HIGHWAY, BUT A 12-POINT BUCK IS A 12-POINT BUCK!

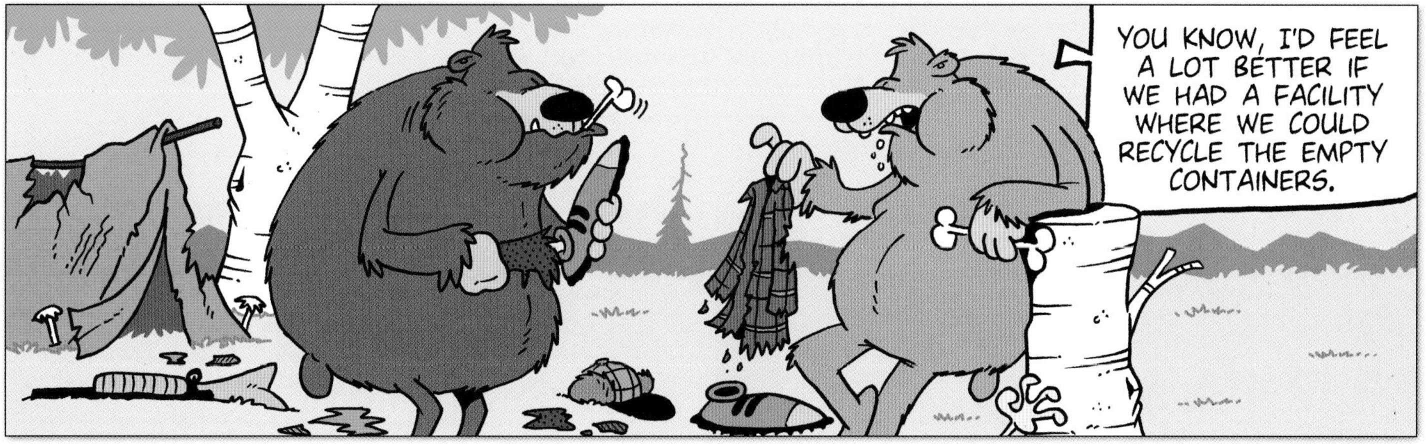
YOU KNOW, I'D FEEL A LOT BETTER IF WE HAD A FACILITY WHERE WE COULD RECYCLE THE EMPTY CONTAINERS.

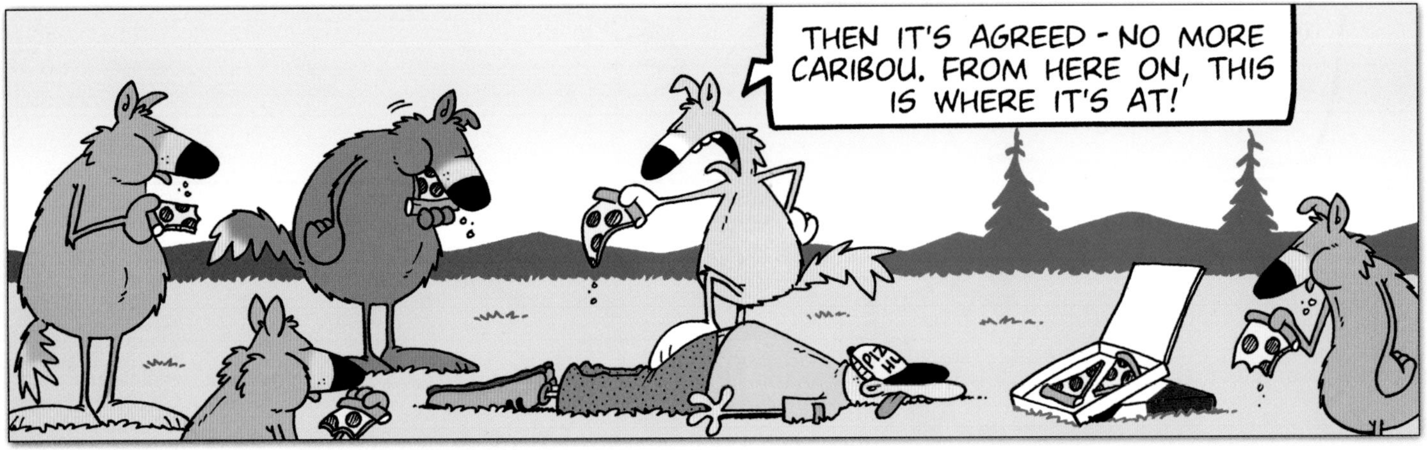
THEN IT'S AGREED - NO MORE CARIBOU. FROM HERE ON, THIS IS WHERE IT'S AT!

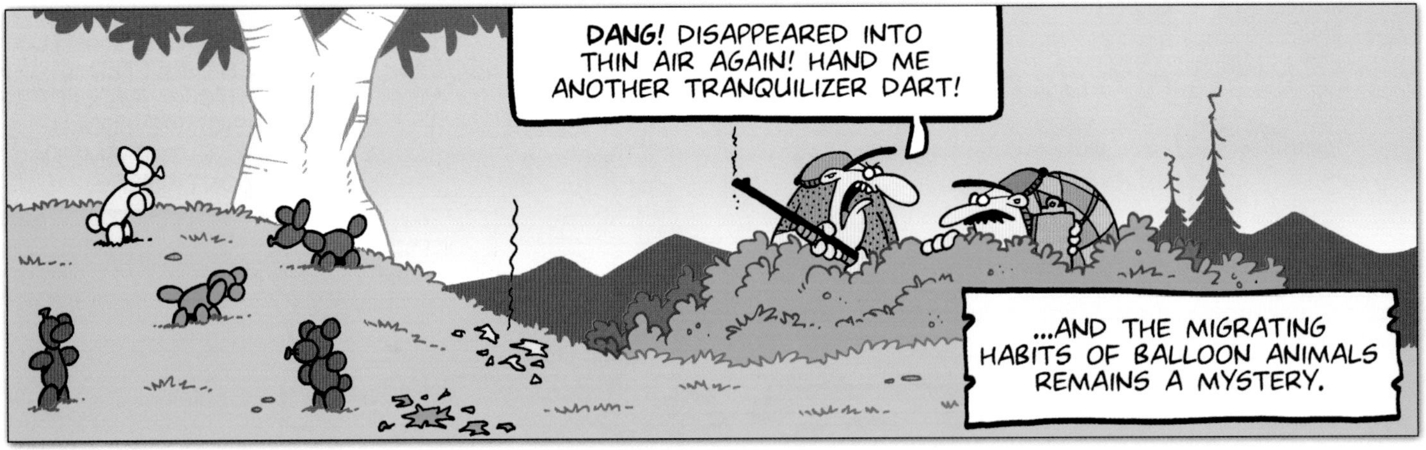
DANG! DISAPPEARED INTO THIN AIR AGAIN! HAND ME ANOTHER TRANQUILIZER DART!
...AND THE MIGRATING HABITS OF BALLOON ANIMALS REMAINS A MYSTERY.

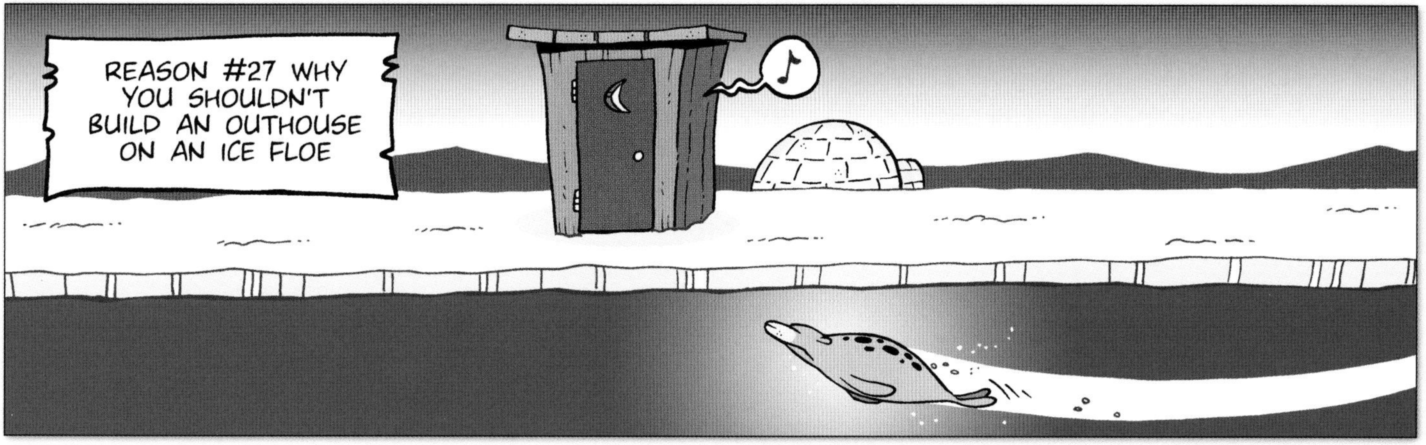
REASON #27 WHY YOU SHOULDN'T BUILD AN OUTHOUSE ON AN ICE FLOE

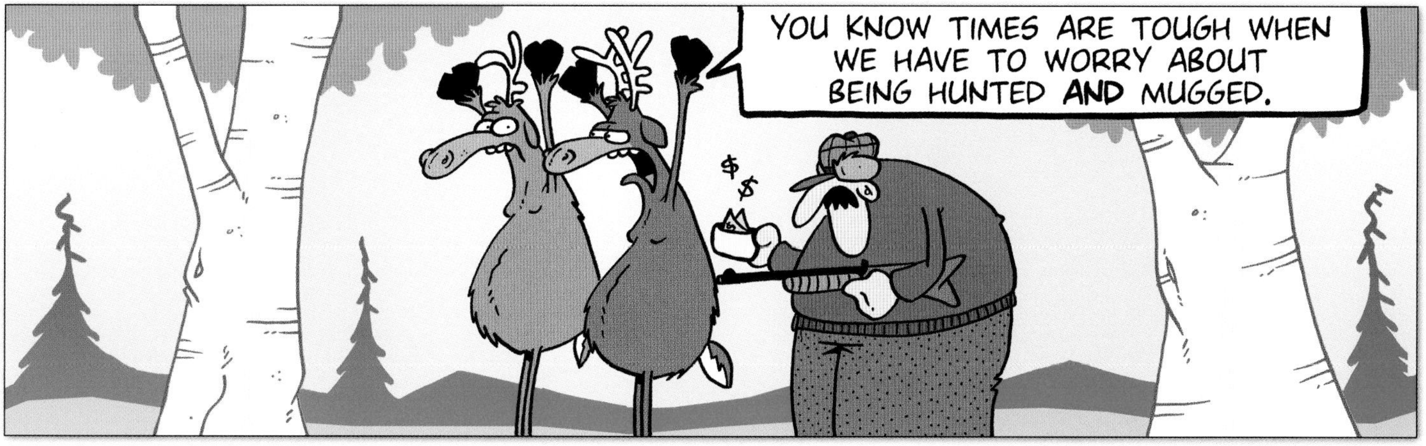
YOU KNOW TIMES ARE TOUGH WHEN WE HAVE TO WORRY ABOUT BEING HUNTED AND MUGGED.
$ $

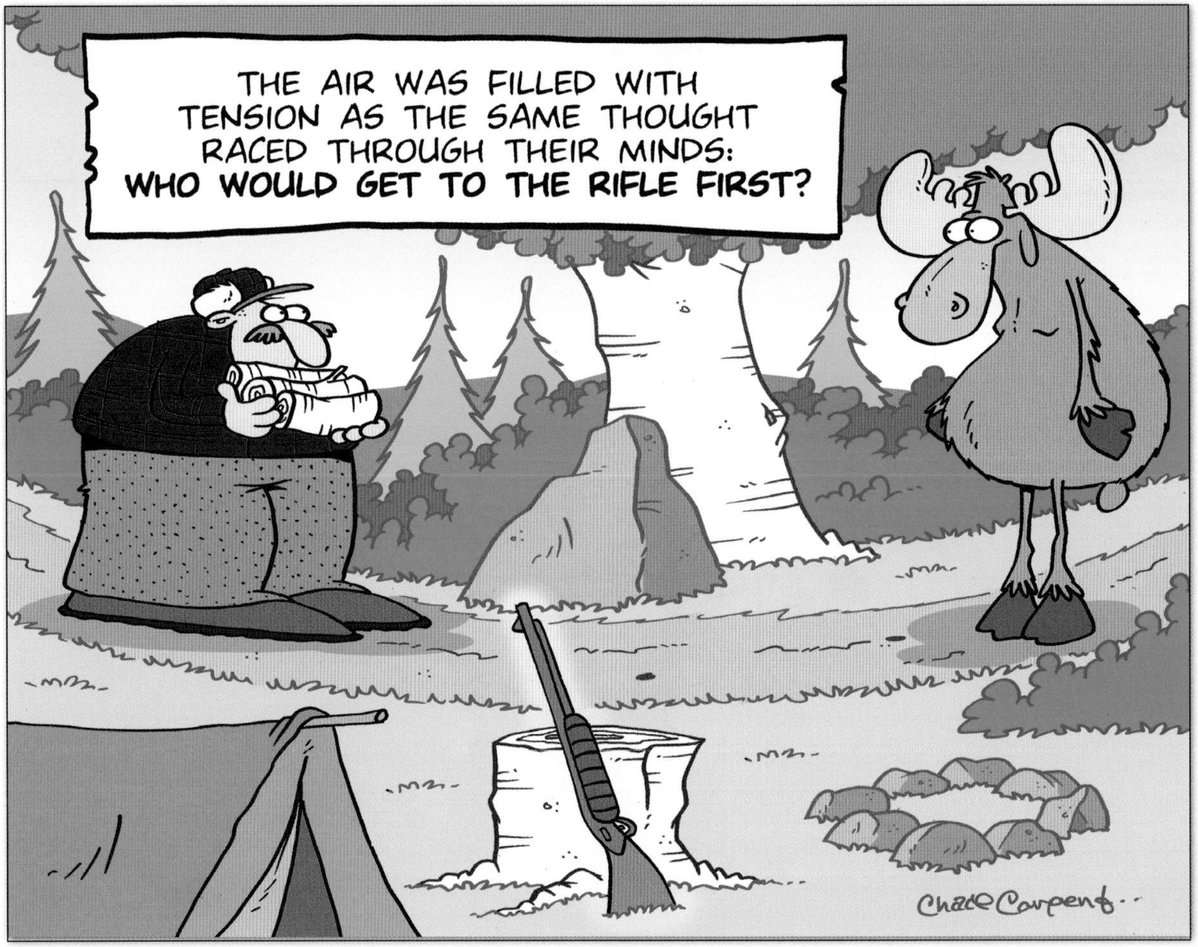
THE AIR WAS FILLED WITH TENSION AS THE SAME THOUGHT RACED THROUGH THEIR MINDS: **WHO WOULD GET TO THE RIFLE FIRST?**

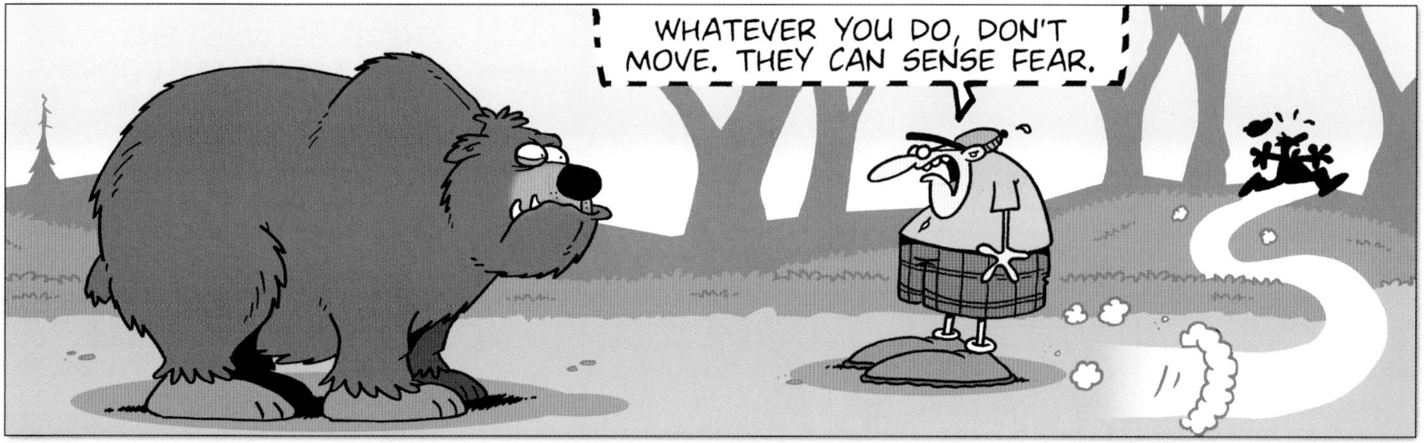
WHATEVER YOU DO, DON'T MOVE. THEY CAN SENSE FEAR.

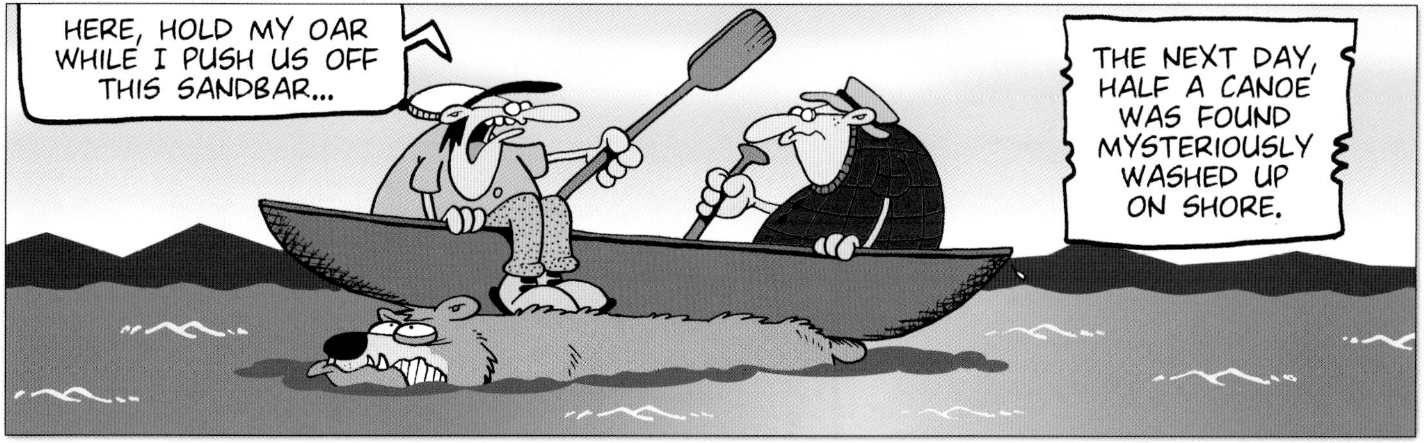
HERE, HOLD MY OAR WHILE I PUSH US OFF THIS SANDBAR...
THE NEXT DAY, HALF A CANOE WAS FOUND MYSTERIOUSLY WASHED UP ON SHORE.

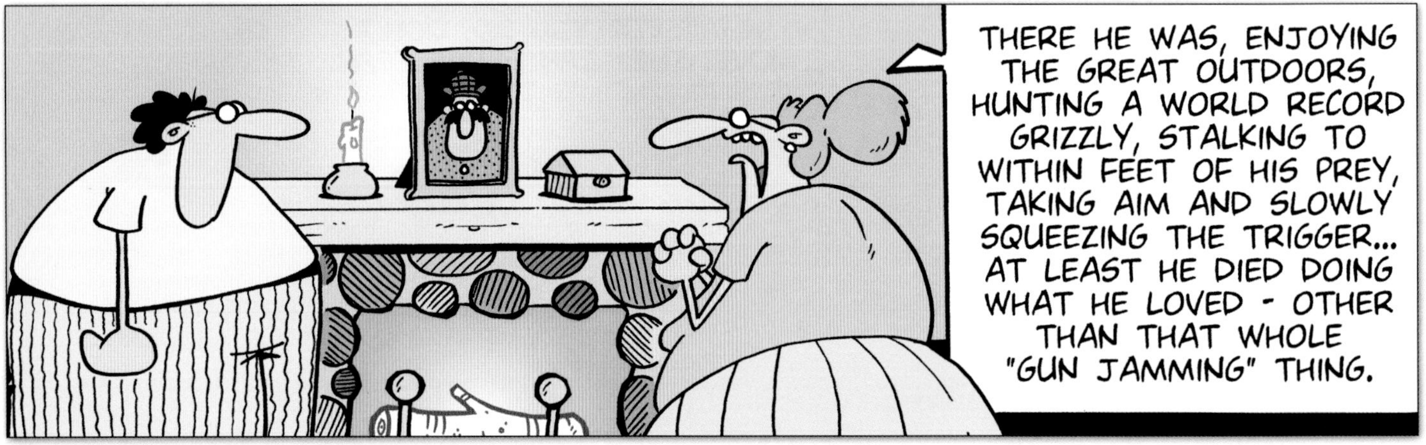
THERE HE WAS, ENJOYING THE GREAT OUTDOORS, HUNTING A WORLD RECORD GRIZZLY, STALKING TO WITHIN FEET OF HIS PREY, TAKING AIM AND SLOWLY SQUEEZING THE TRIGGER... AT LEAST HE DIED DOING WHAT HE LOVED - OTHER THAN THAT WHOLE "GUN JAMMING" THING.

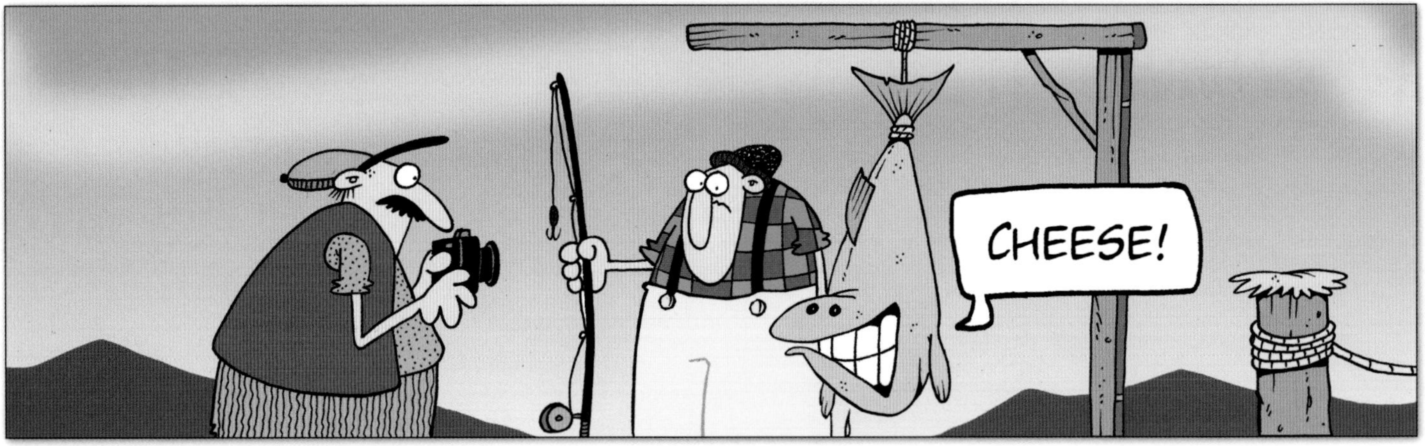
CHEESE!

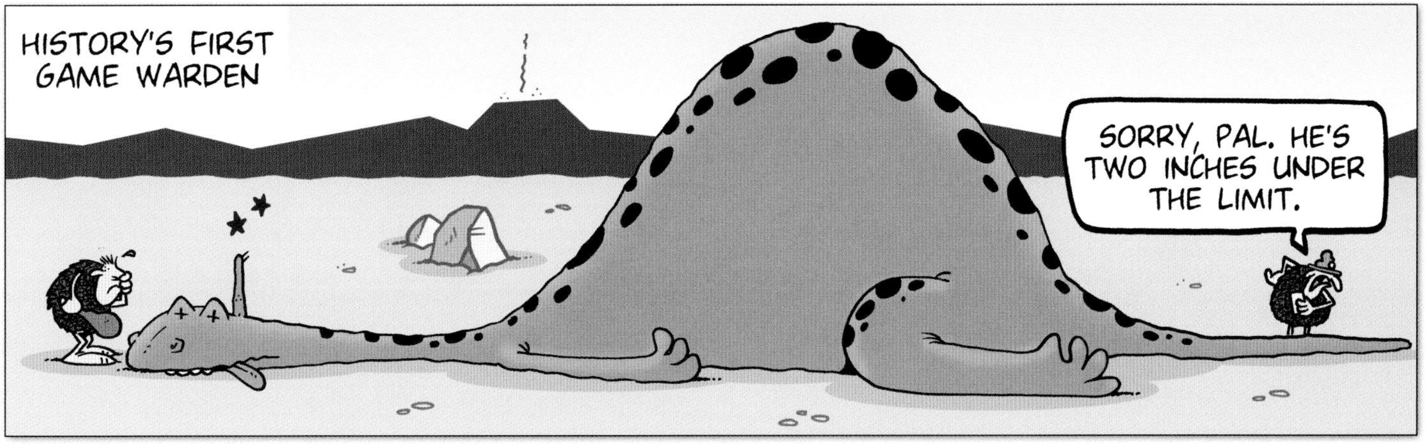
HISTORY'S FIRST GAME WARDEN
SORRY, PAL. HE'S TWO INCHES UNDER THE LIMIT.

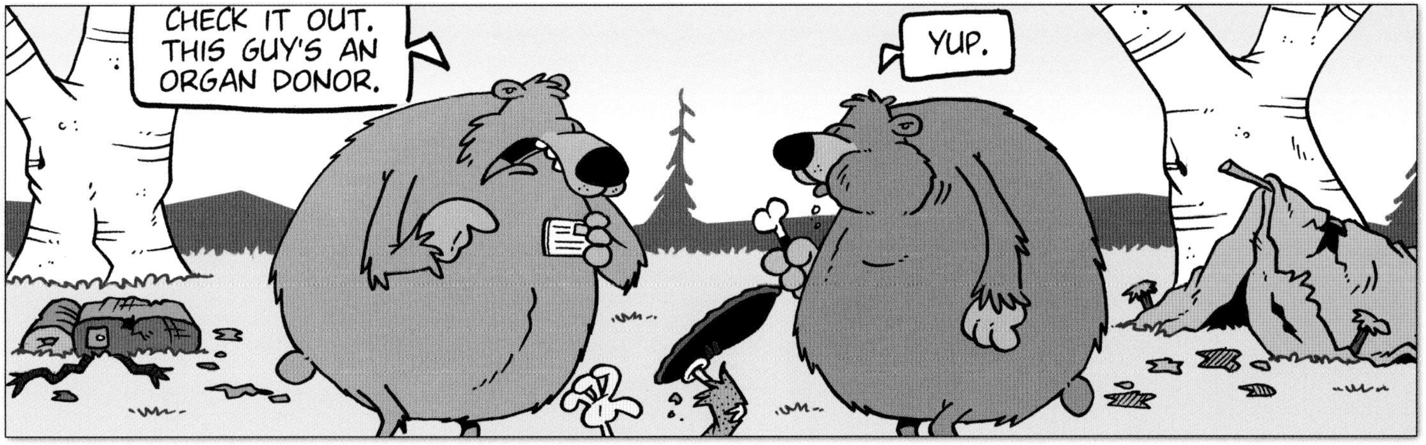
CHECK IT OUT. THIS GUY'S AN ORGAN DONOR.
YUP.

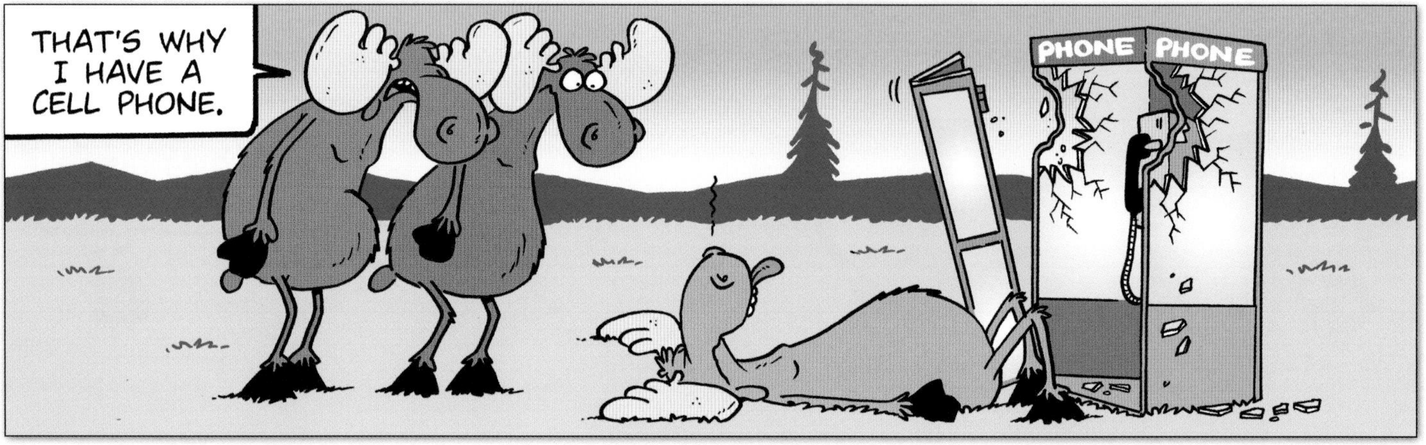
THAT'S WHY I HAVE A CELL PHONE.
PHONE
PHONE

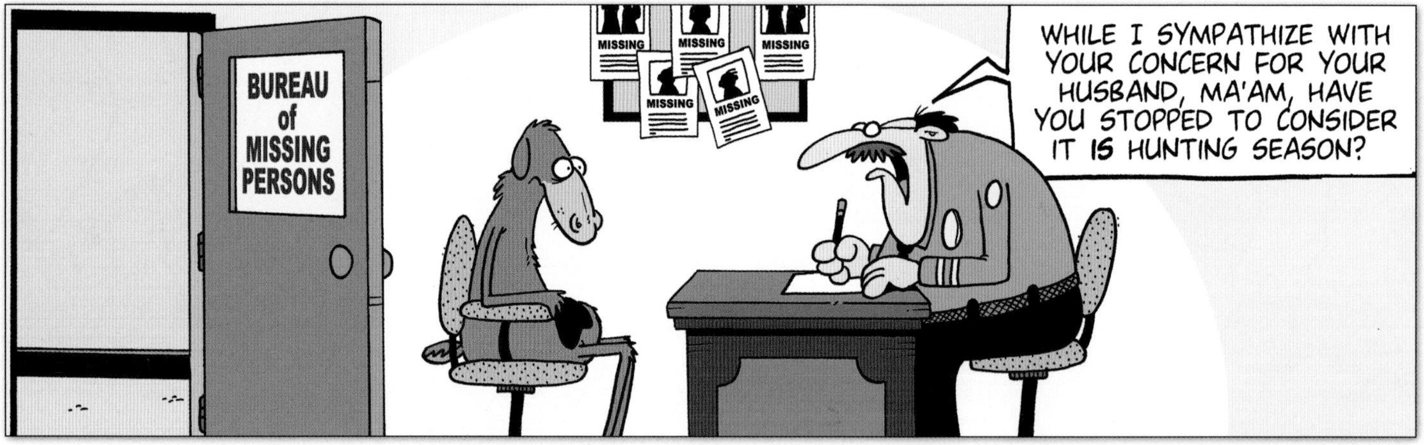
BUREAU of MISSING PERSONS
MISSING
MISSING
MISSING
MISSING
MISSING
WHILE I SYMPATHIZE WITH YOUR CONCERN FOR YOUR HUSBAND, MA'AM, HAVE YOU STOPPED TO CONSIDER IT **IS** HUNTING SEASON?

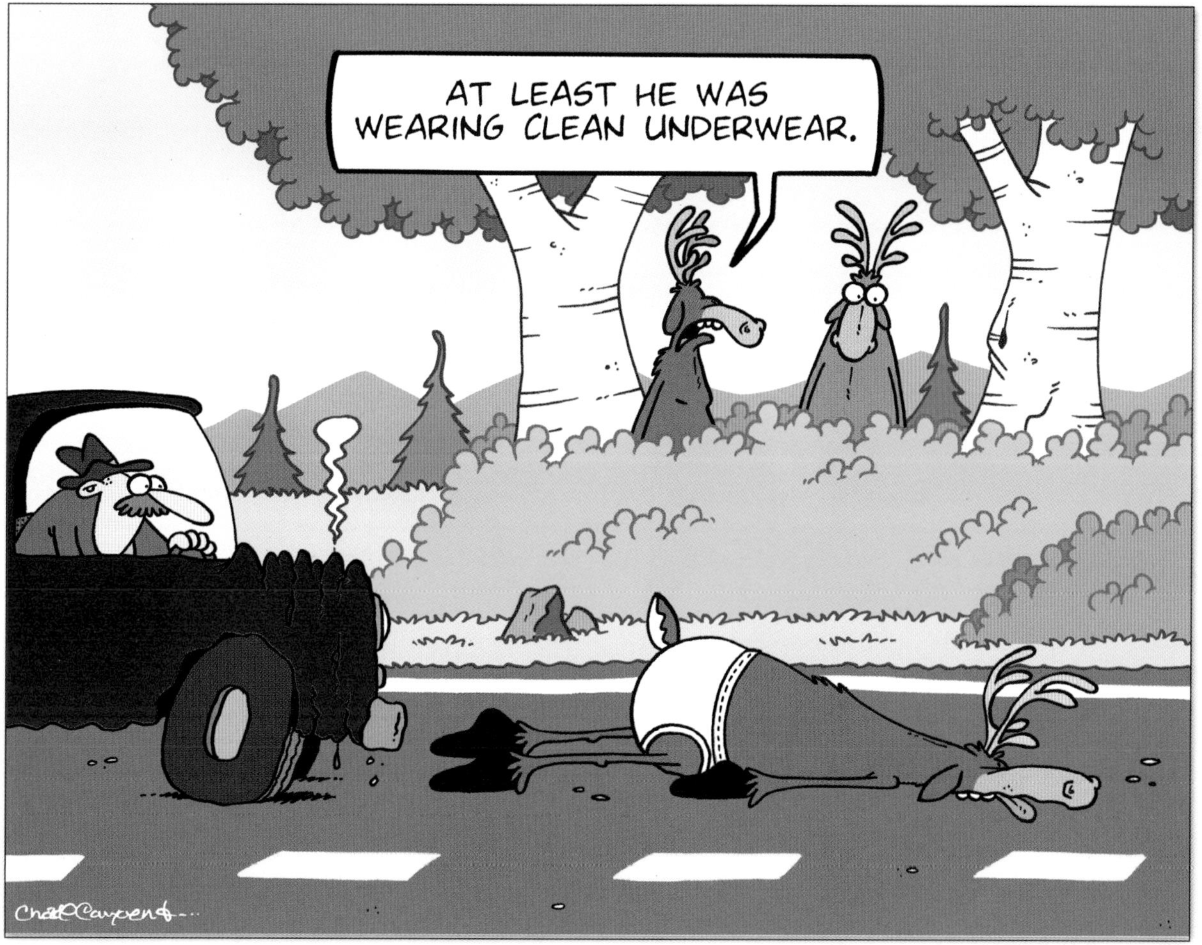
AT LEAST HE WAS WEARING CLEAN UNDERWEAR.

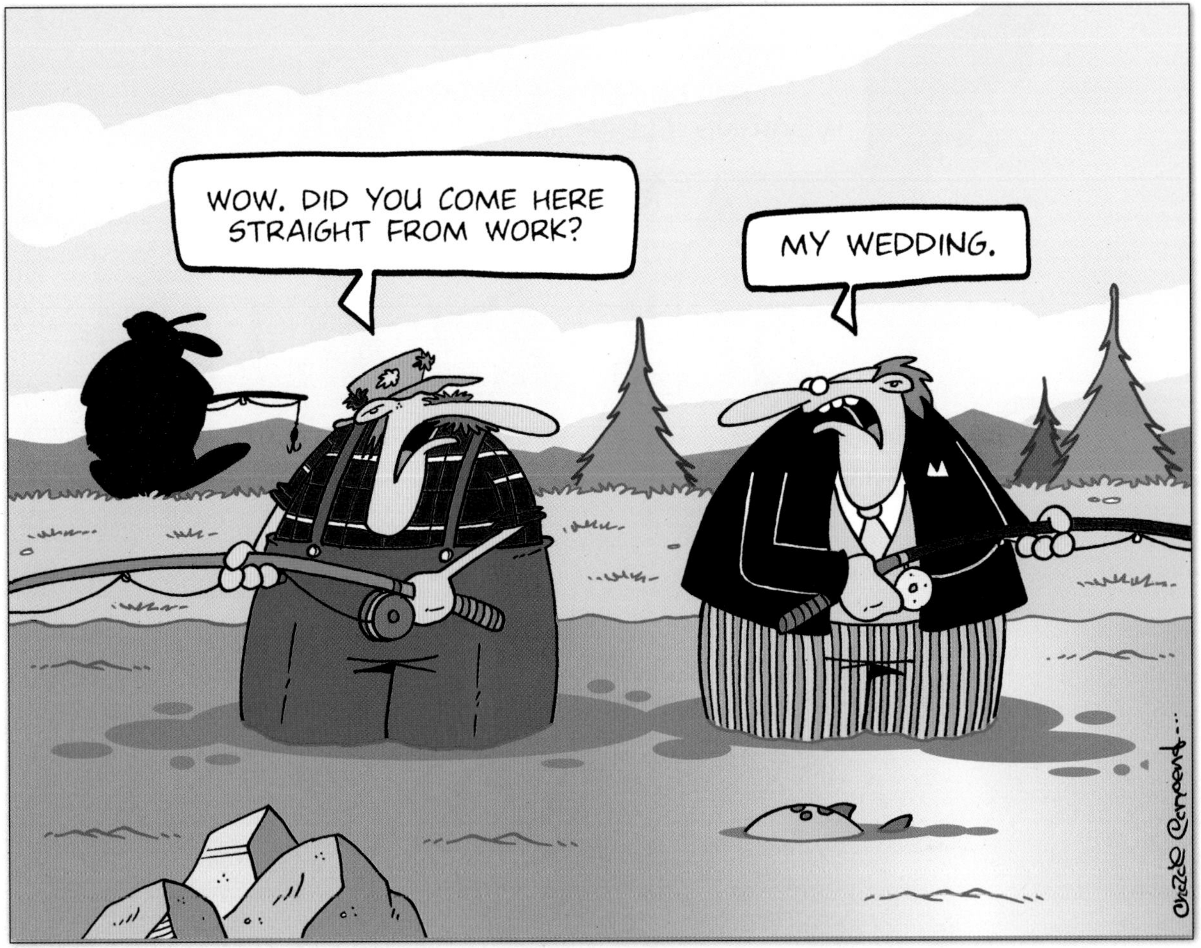
WOW. DID YOU COME HERE STRAIGHT FROM WORK?
MY WEDDING.

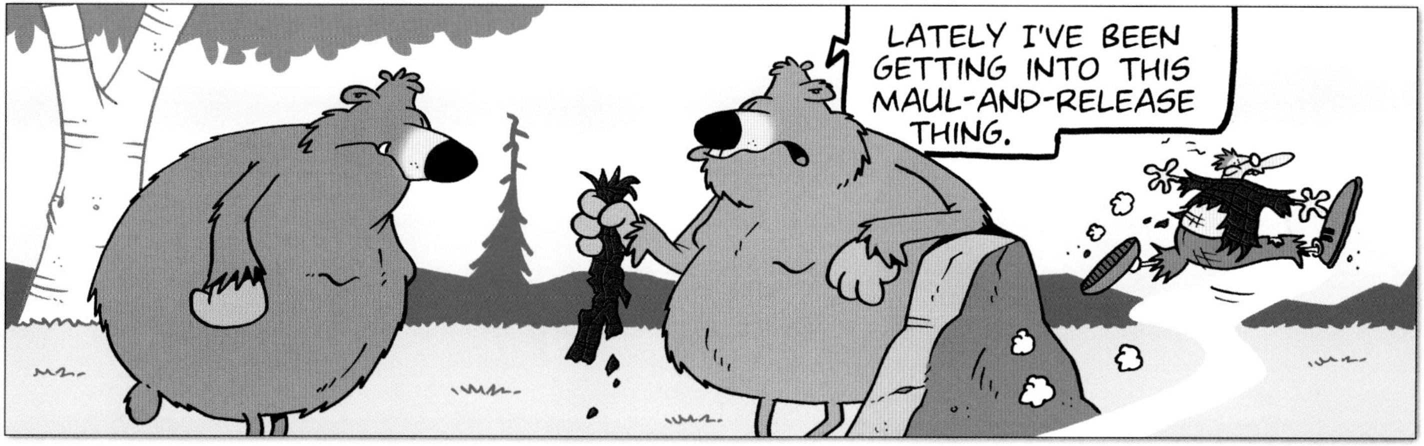
LATELY I'VE BEEN GETTING INTO THIS MAUL-AND-RELEASE THING.

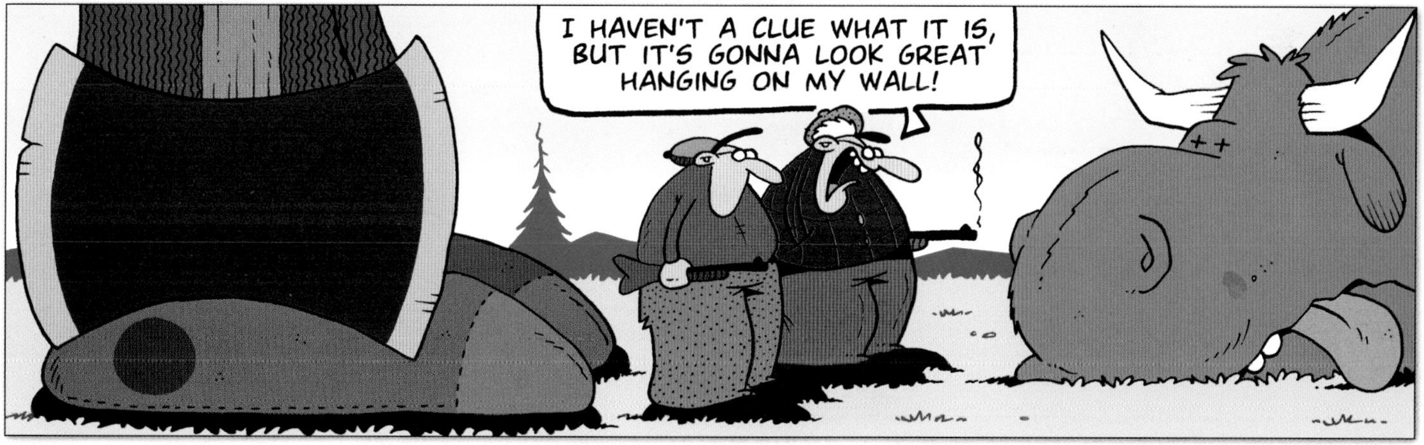
I HAVEN'T A CLUE WHAT IT IS, BUT IT'S GONNA LOOK GREAT HANGING ON MY WALL!

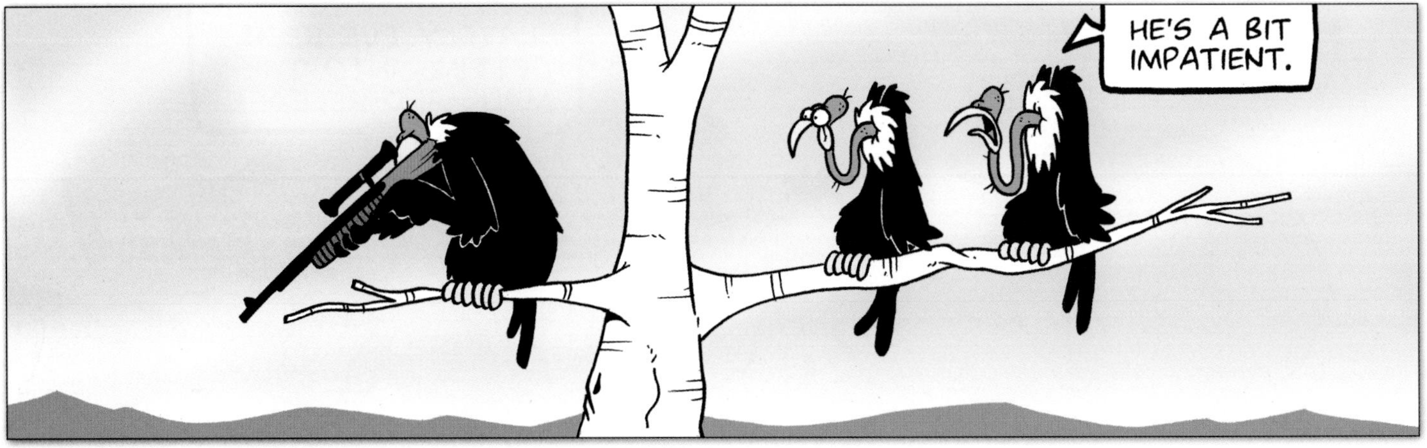
HE'S A BIT IMPATIENT.

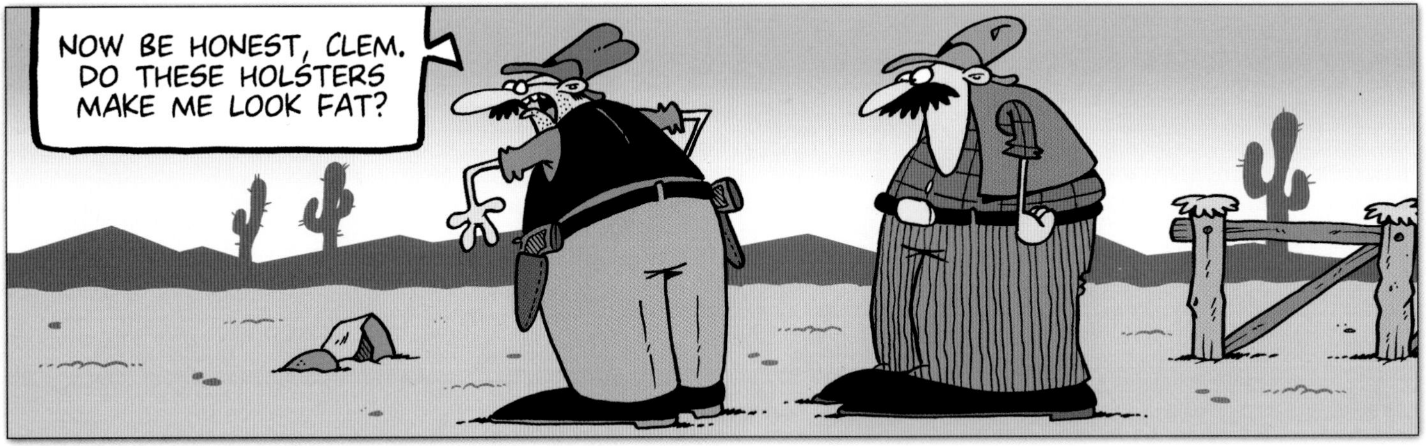
NOW BE HONEST, CLEM. DO THESE HOLSTERS MAKE ME LOOK FAT?

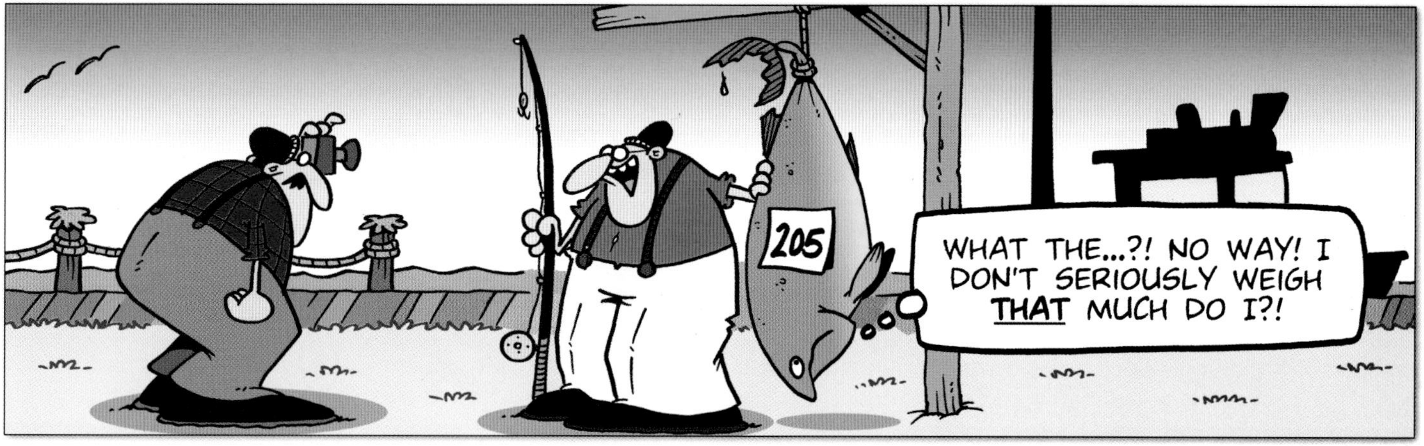
205
WHAT THE...?! NO WAY! I DON'T SERIOUSLY WEIGH THAT MUCH DO I?!

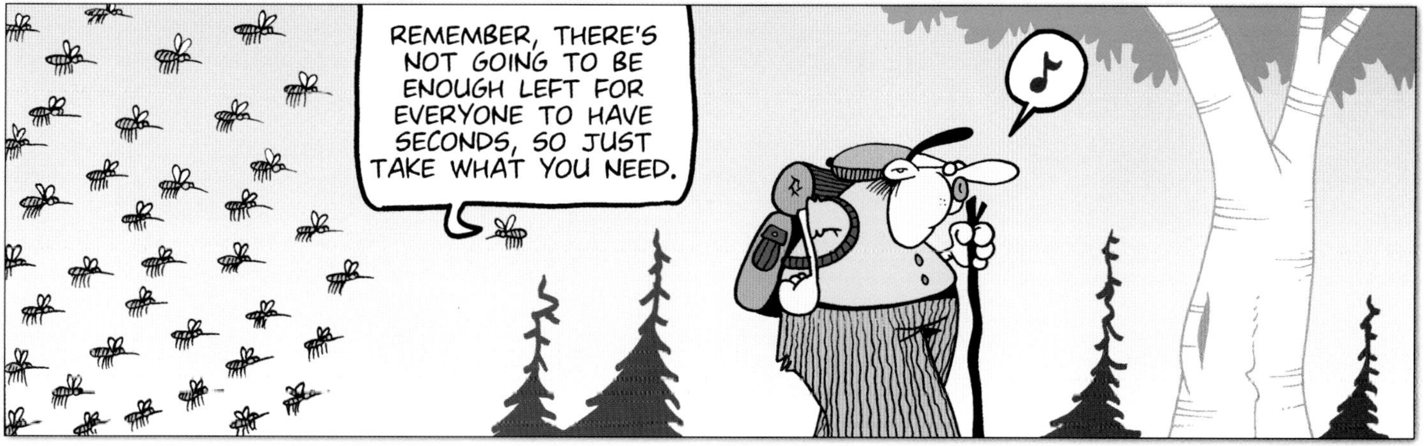
REMEMBER, THERE'S NOT GOING TO BE ENOUGH LEFT FOR EVERYONE TO HAVE SECONDS, SO JUST TAKE WHAT YOU NEED.

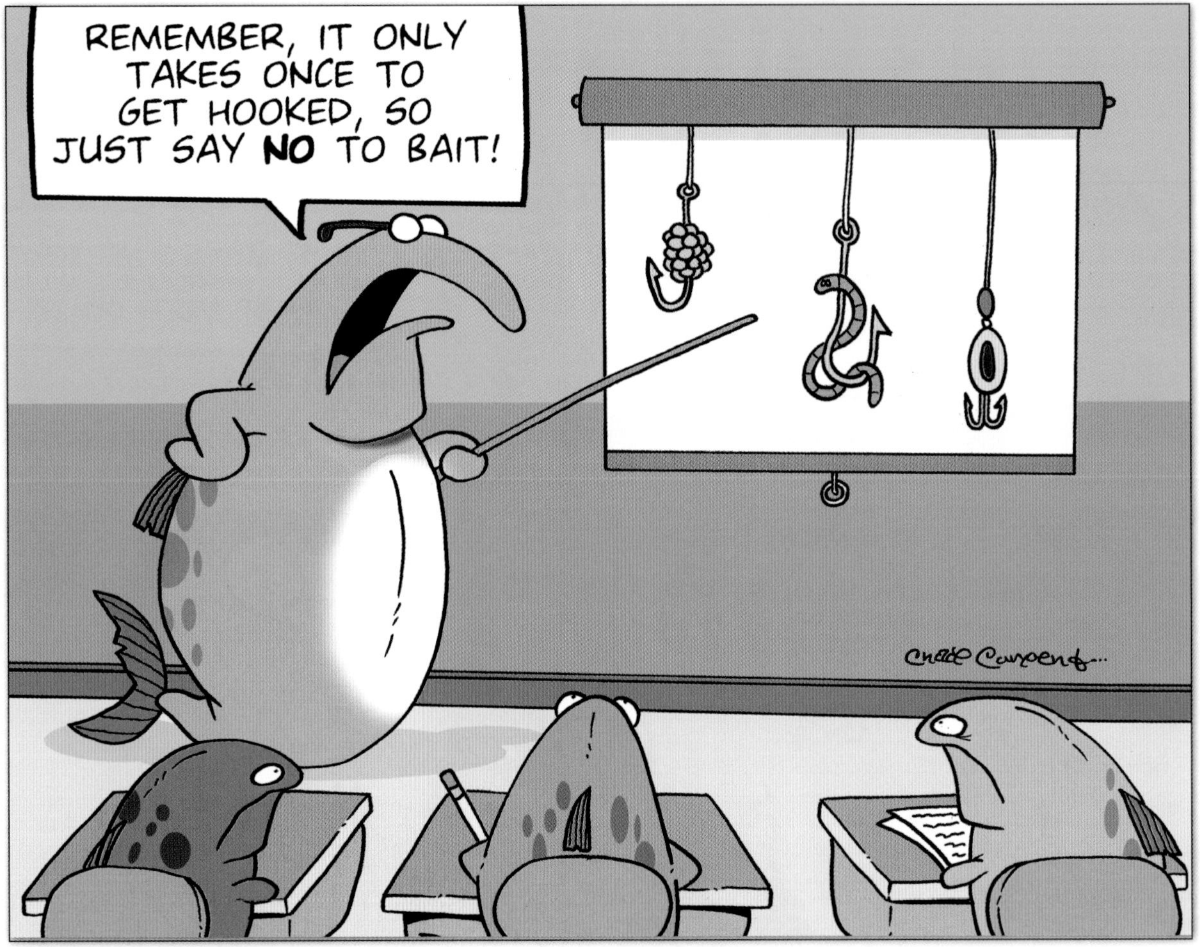
REMEMBER, IT ONLY TAKES ONCE TO GET HOOKED, SO JUST SAY **NO** TO BAIT!

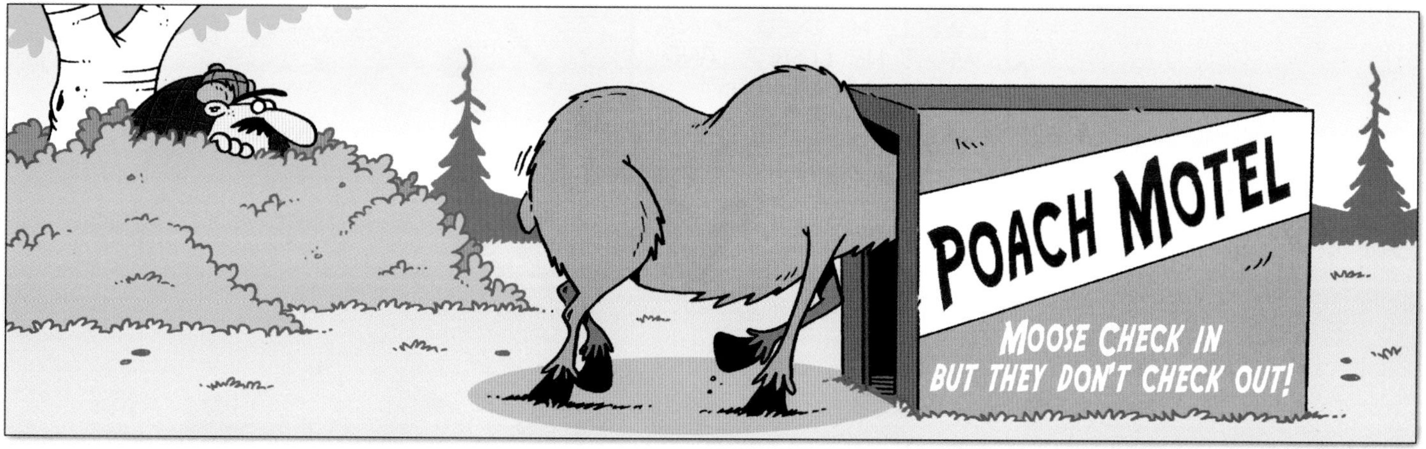
POACH MOTEL
MOOSE CHECK IN BUT THEY DON'T CHECK OUT!

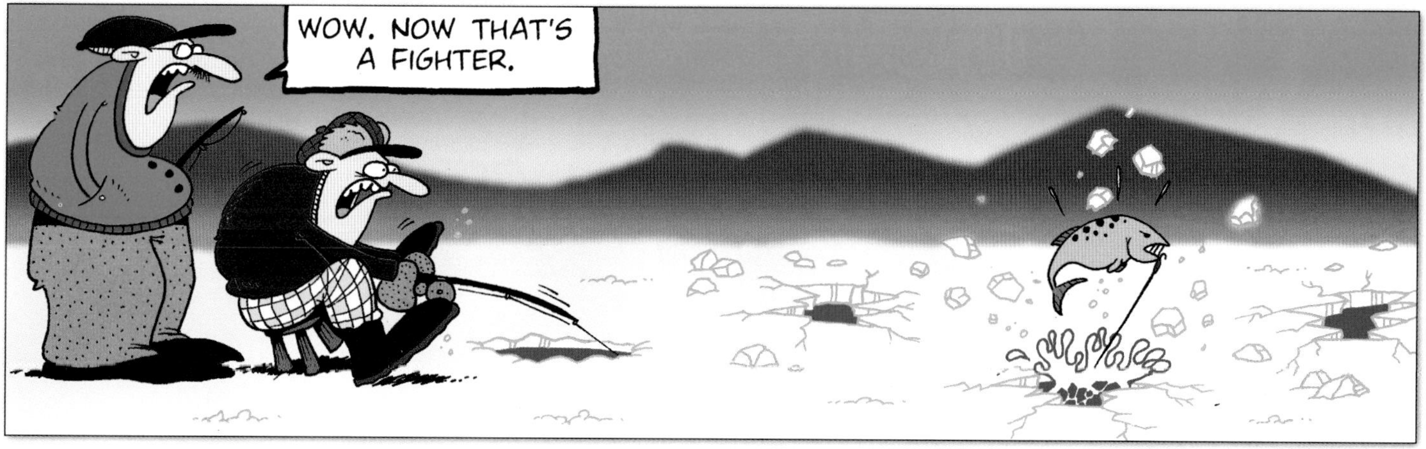
WOW. NOW THAT'S A FIGHTER.

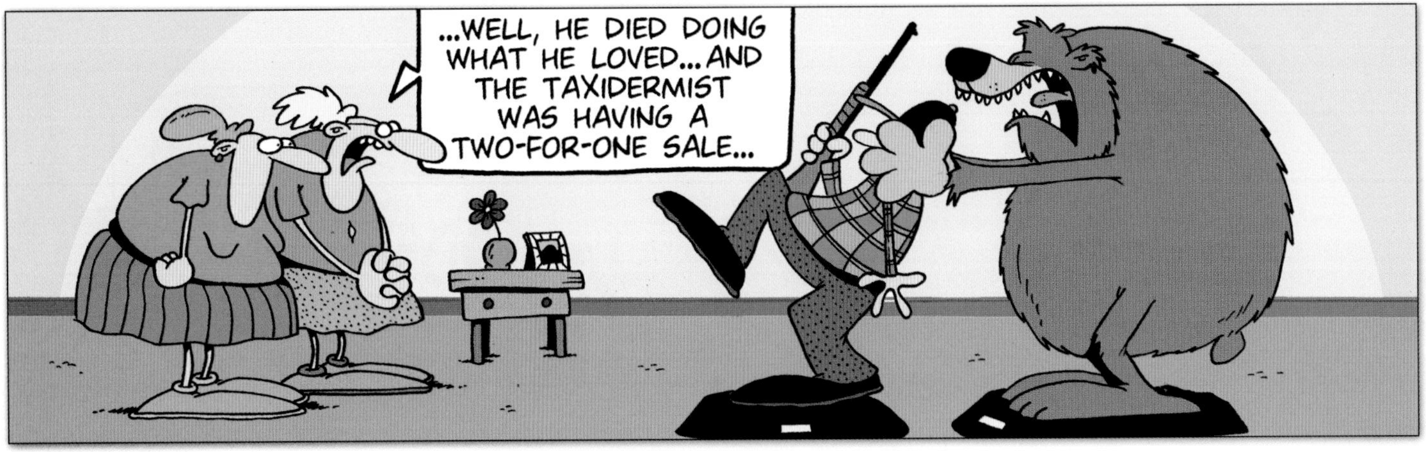
...WELL, HE DIED DOING WHAT HE LOVED...AND THE TAXIDERMIST WAS HAVING A TWO-FOR-ONE SALE...

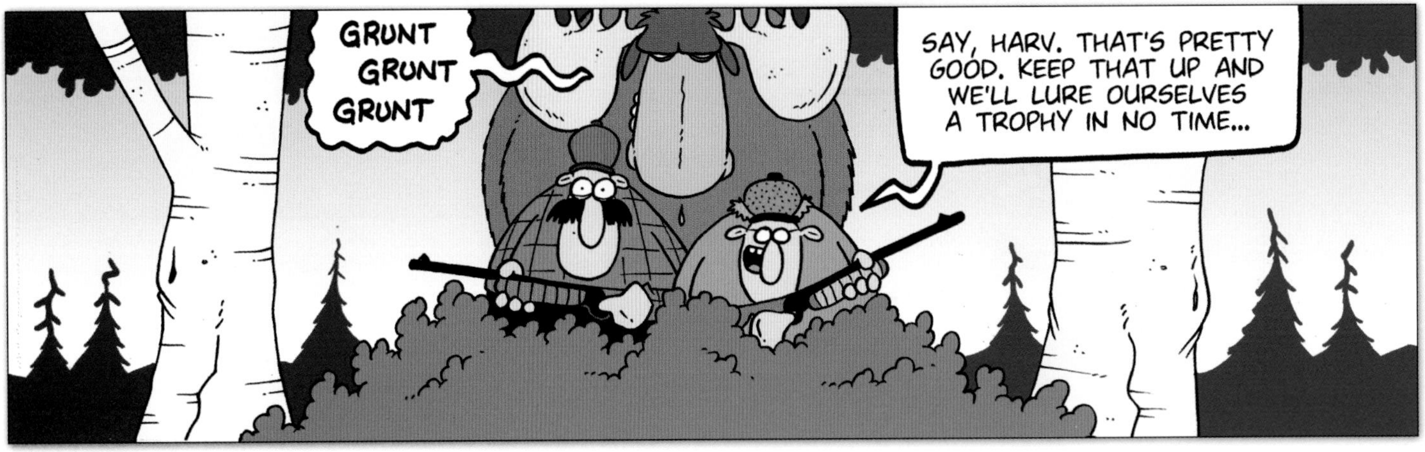
GRUNT GRUNT GRUNT
SAY, HARV. THAT'S PRETTY GOOD. KEEP THAT UP AND WE'LL LURE OURSELVES A TROPHY IN NO TIME...

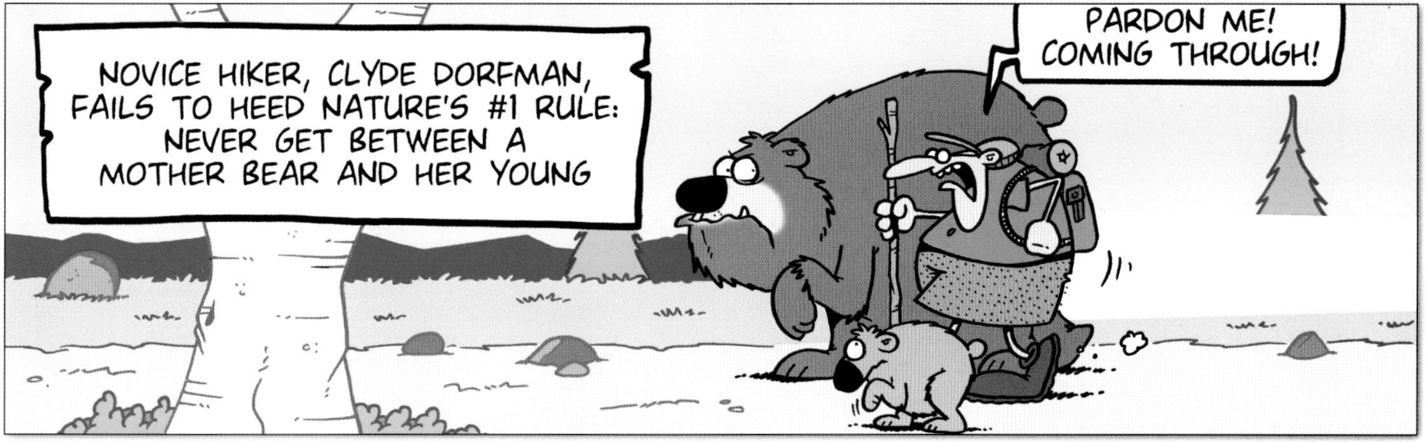
NOVICE HIKER, CLYDE DORFMAN, FAILS TO HEED NATURE'S #1 RULE: NEVER GET BETWEEN A MOTHER BEAR AND HER YOUNG
PARDON ME! COMING THROUGH!

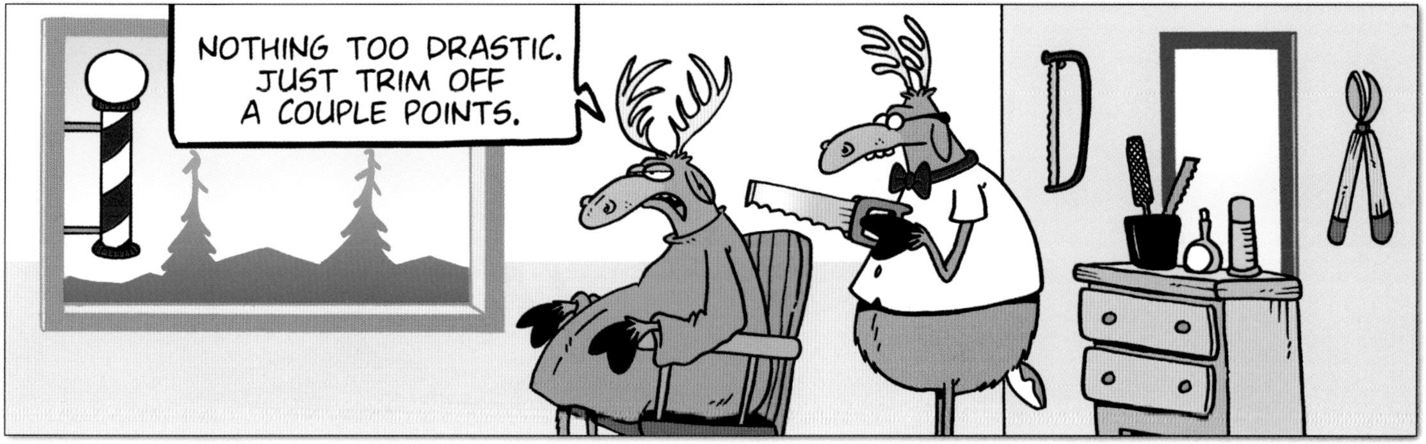
NOTHING TOO DRASTIC. JUST TRIM OFF A COUPLE POINTS.

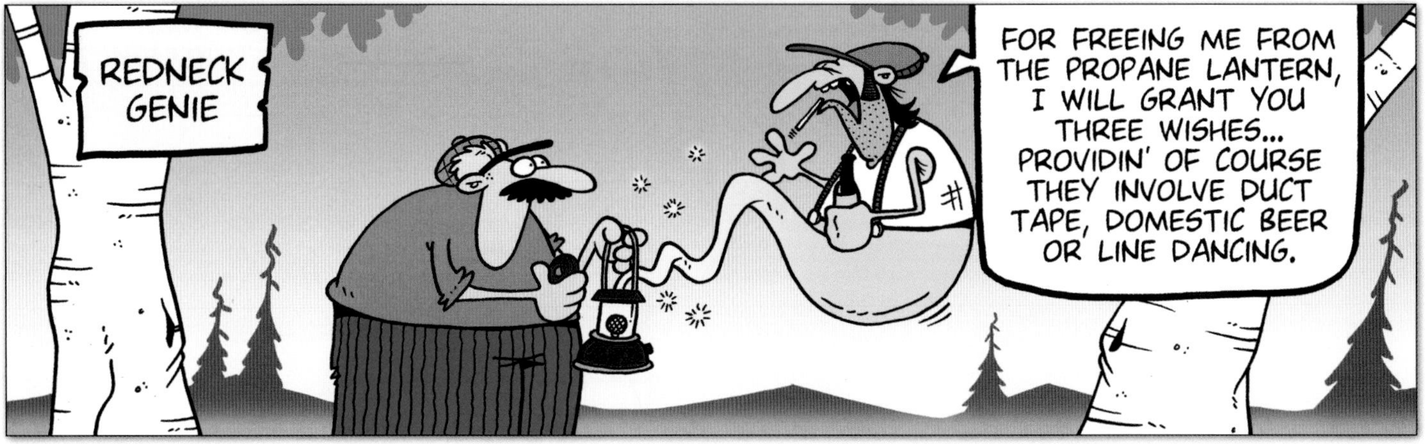
REDNECK GENIE
FOR FREEING ME FROM THE PROPANE LANTERN, I WILL GRANT YOU THREE WISHES... PROVIDIN' OF COURSE THEY INVOLVE DUCT TAPE, DOMESTIC BEER OR LINE DANCING.

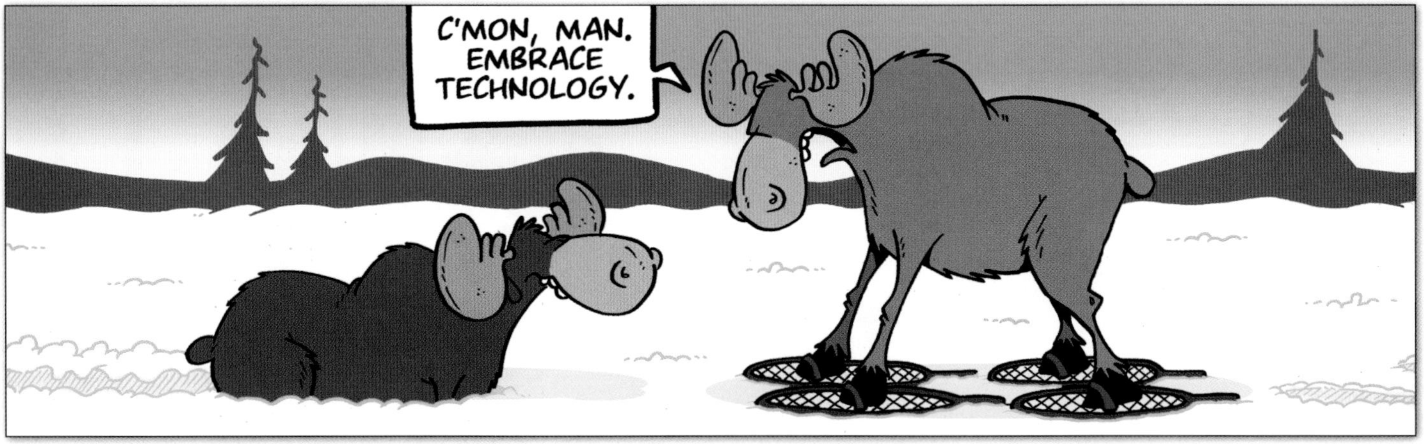
C'MON, MAN. EMBRACE TECHNOLOGY.

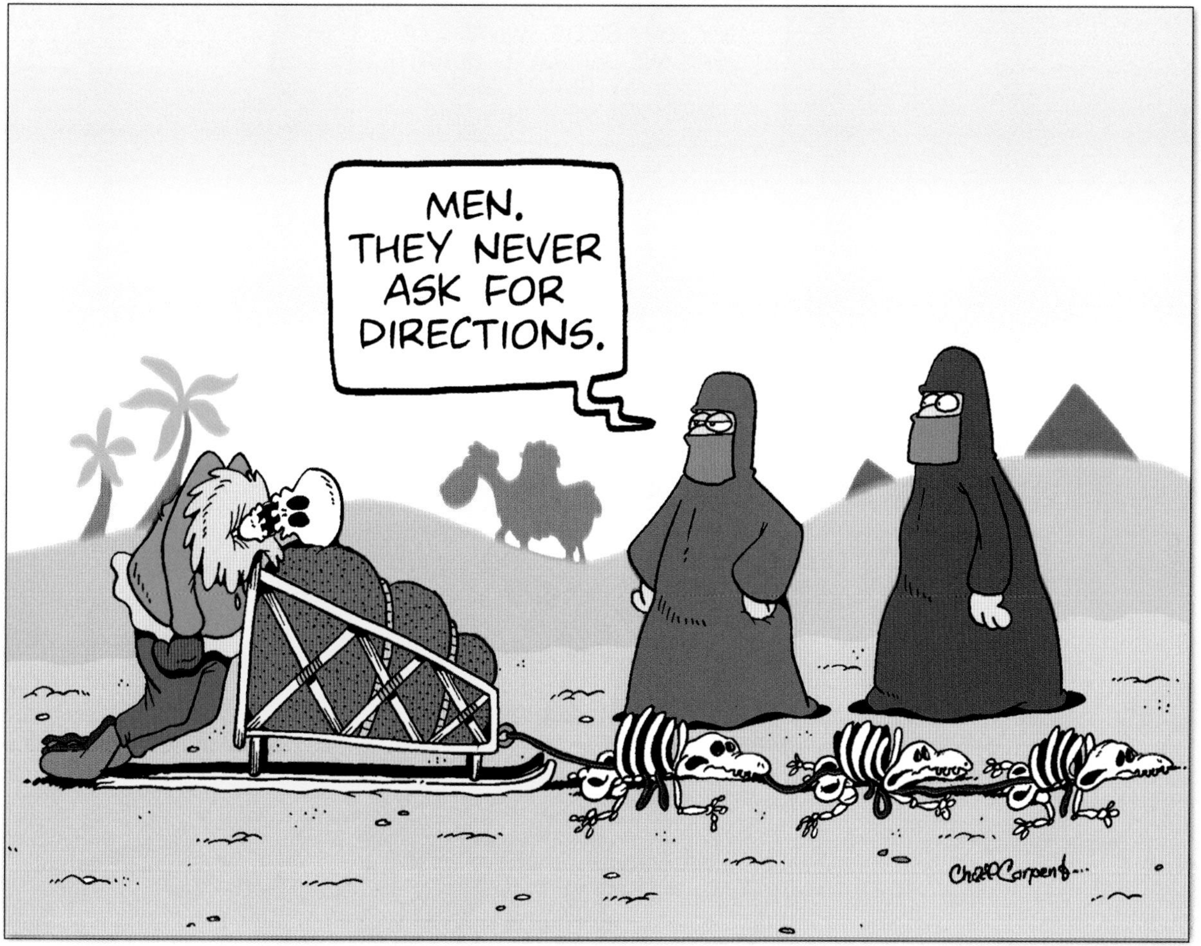
MEN. THEY NEVER ASK FOR DIRECTIONS.

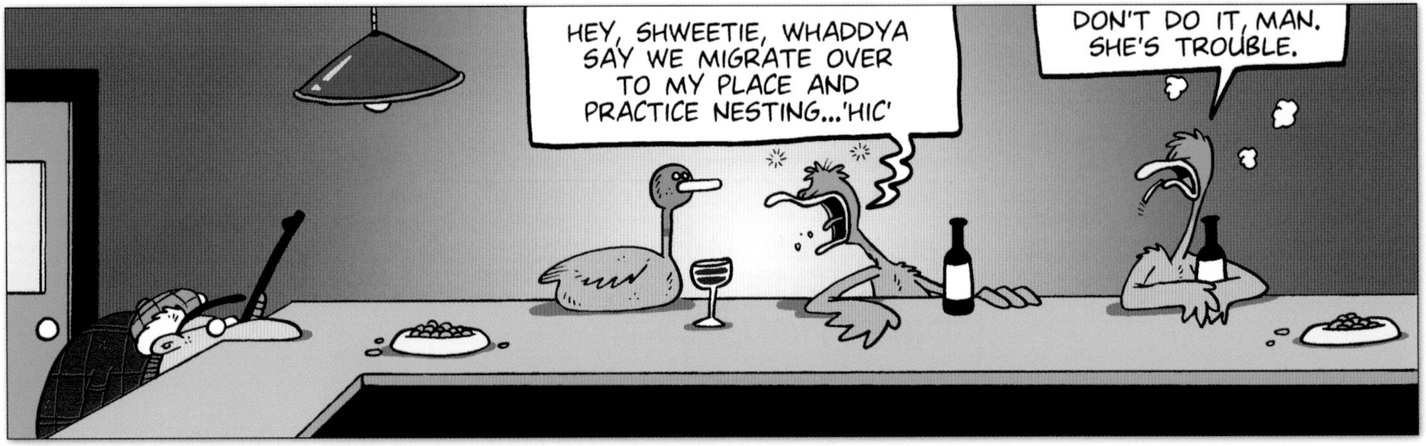
HEY, SHWEETIE, WHADDYA SAY WE MIGRATE OVER TO MY PLACE AND PRACTICE NESTING...'HIC'
DON'T DO IT, MAN. SHE'S TROUBLE.

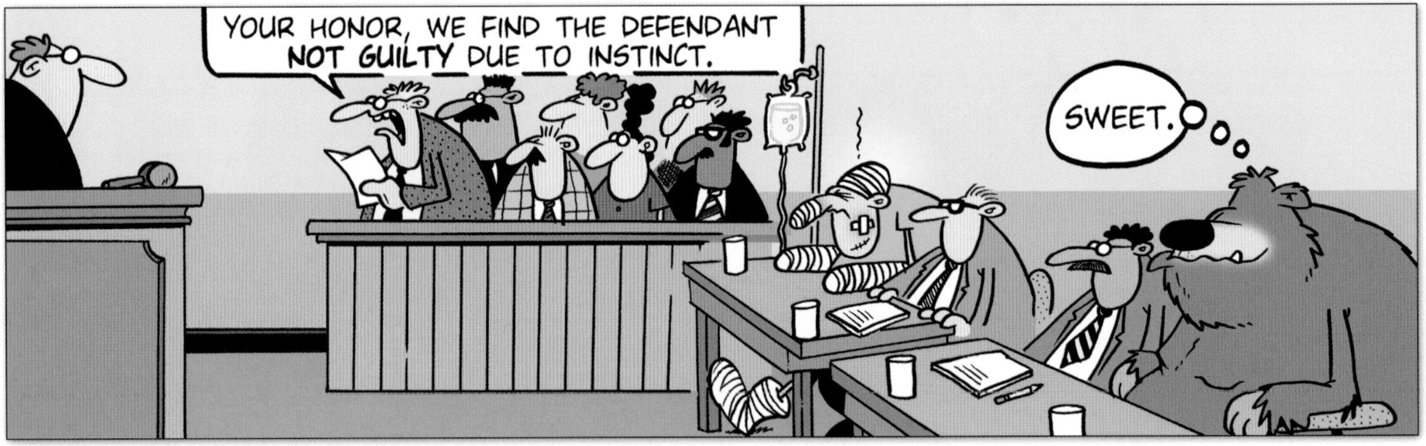
YOUR HONOR, WE FIND THE DEFENDANT **NOT GUILTY** DUE TO INSTINCT.
SWEET.

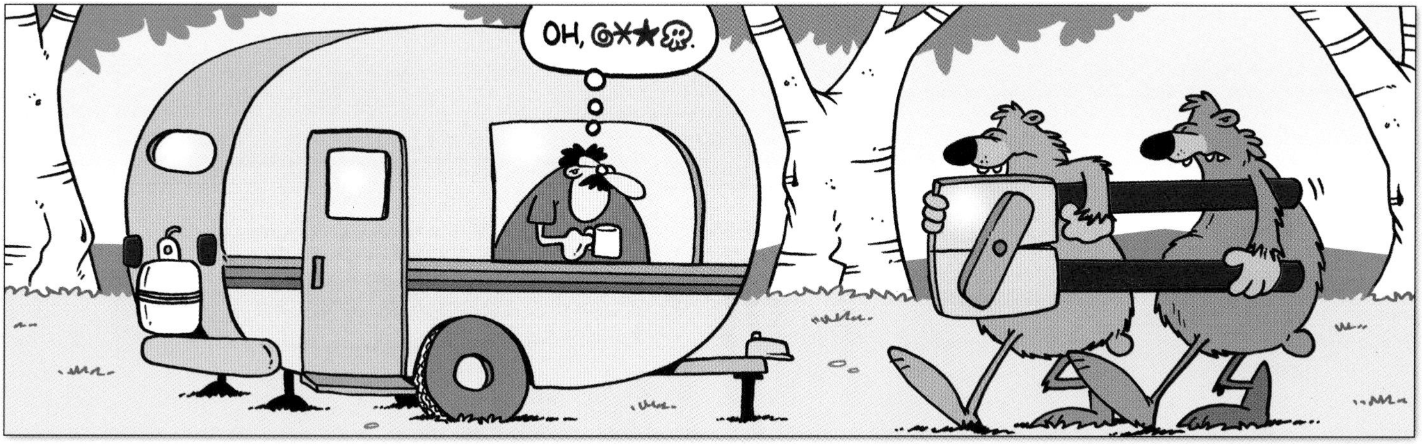
OH, @*★☠.

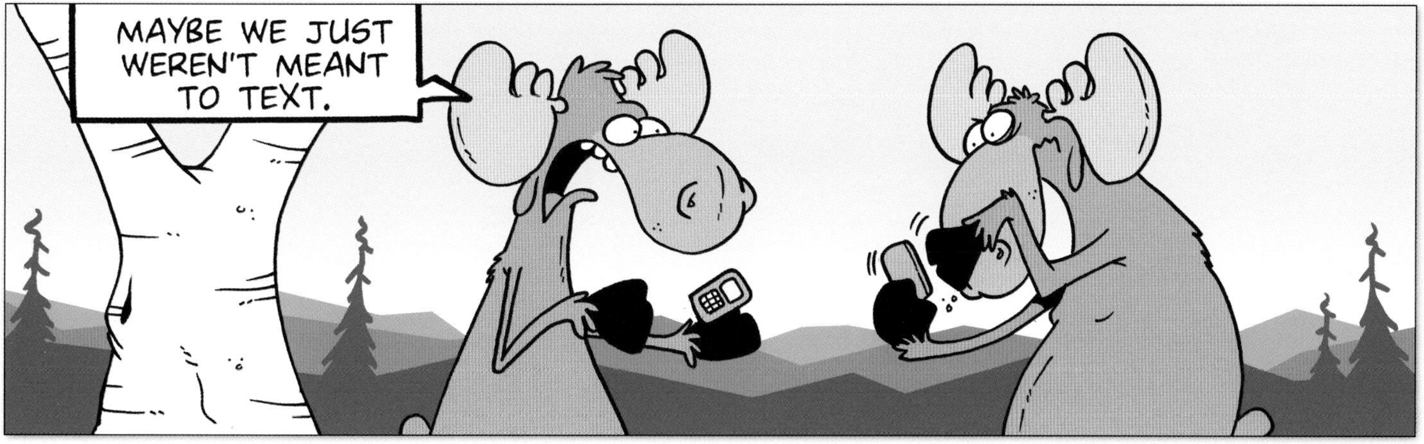
MAYBE WE JUST WEREN'T MEANT TO TEXT.

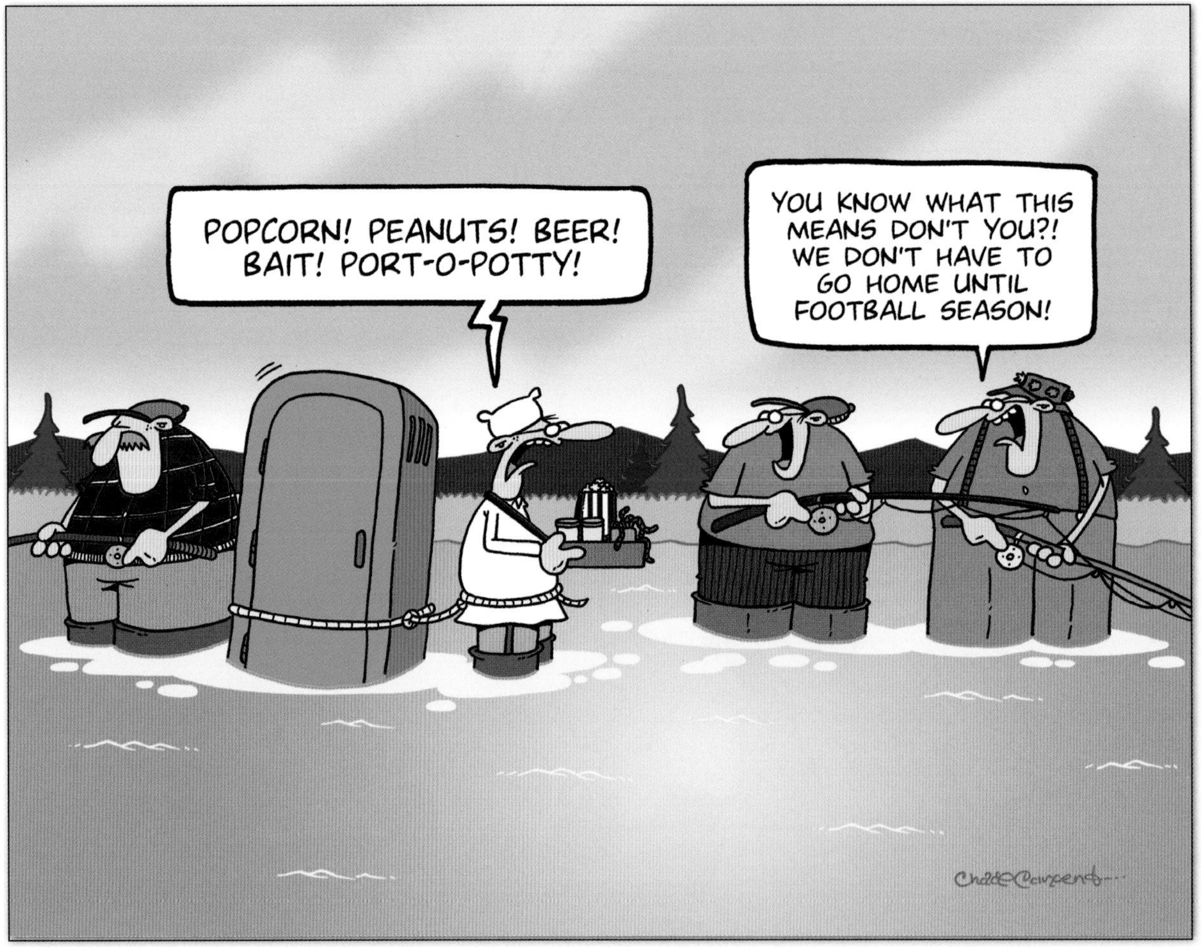
POPCORN! PEANUTS! BEER! BAIT! PORT-O-POTTY!
YOU KNOW WHAT THIS MEANS DON'T YOU?! WE DON'T HAVE TO GO HOME UNTIL FOOTBALL SEASON!

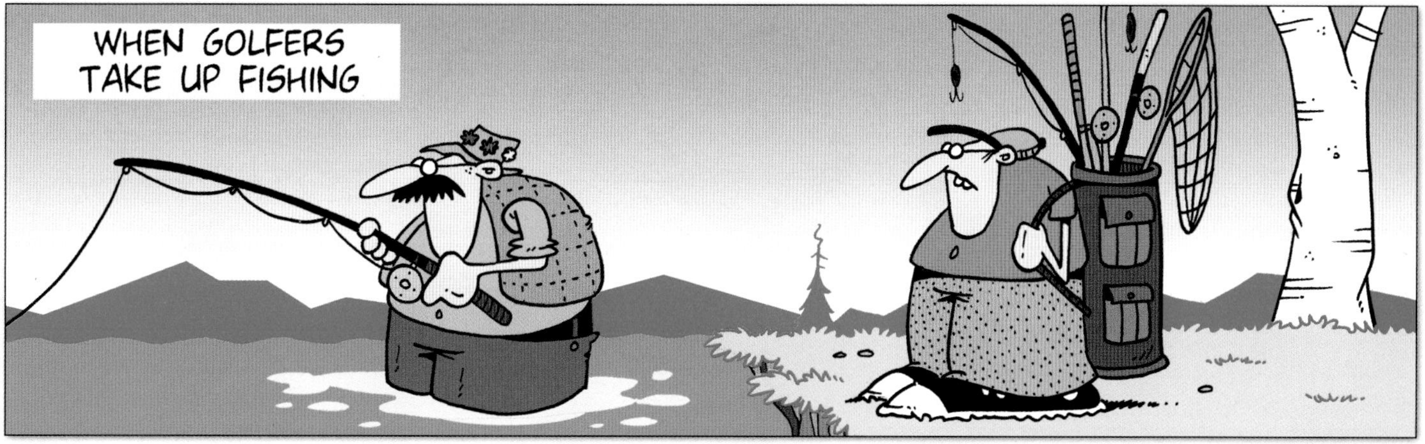
WHEN GOLFERS
TAKE UP FISHING

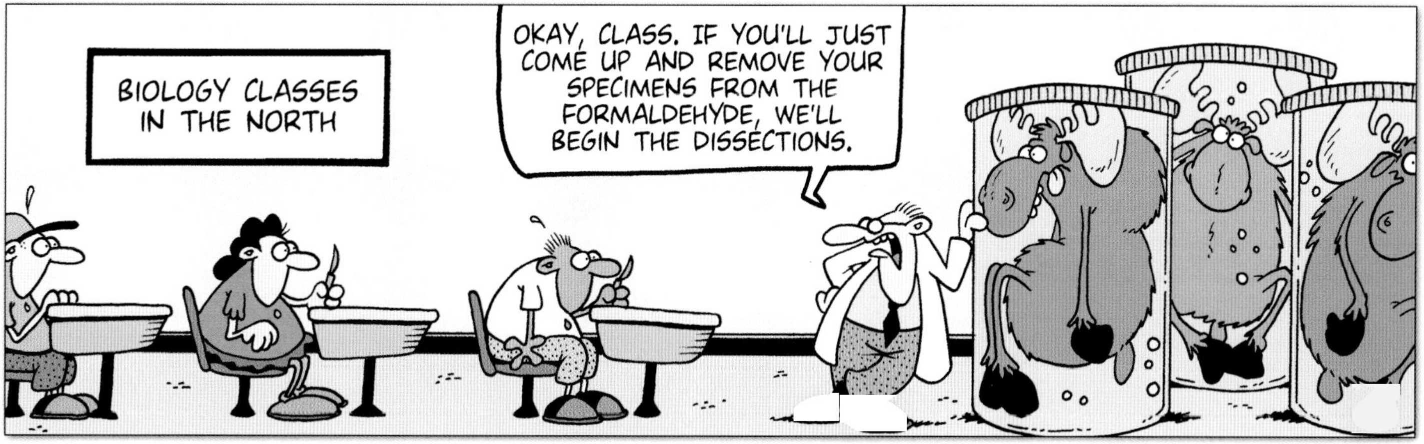
BIOLOGY CLASSES
IN THE NORTH
OKAY, CLASS. IF YOU'LL JUST COME UP AND REMOVE YOUR SPECIMENS FROM THE FORMALDEHYDE, WE'LL BEGIN THE DISSECTIONS.

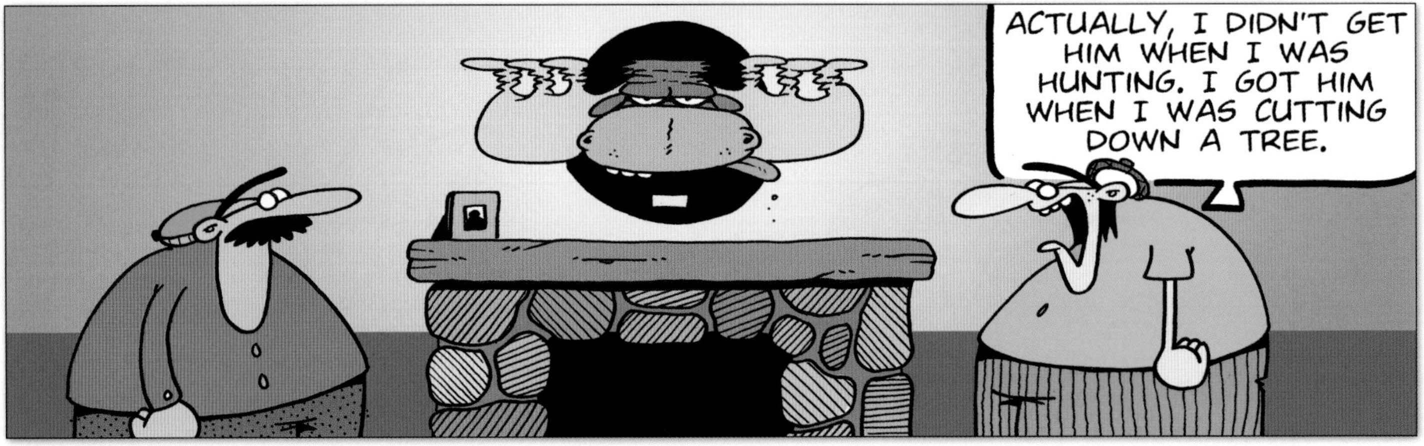
ACTUALLY, I DIDN'T GET HIM WHEN I WAS HUNTING. I GOT HIM WHEN I WAS CUTTING DOWN A TREE.

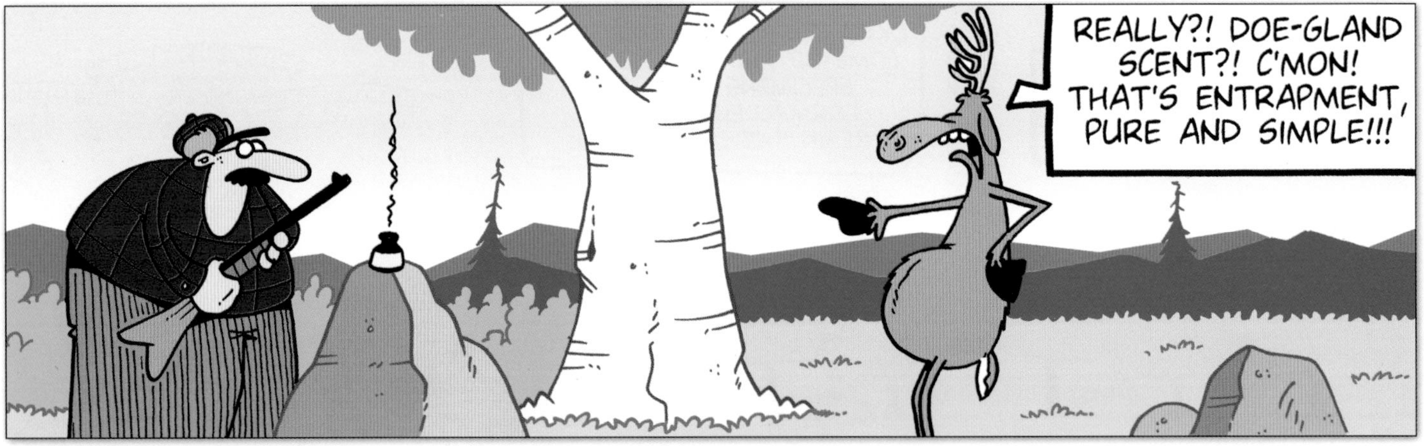
REALLY?! DOE-GLAND SCENT?! C'MON! THAT'S ENTRAPMENT, PURE AND SIMPLE!!!

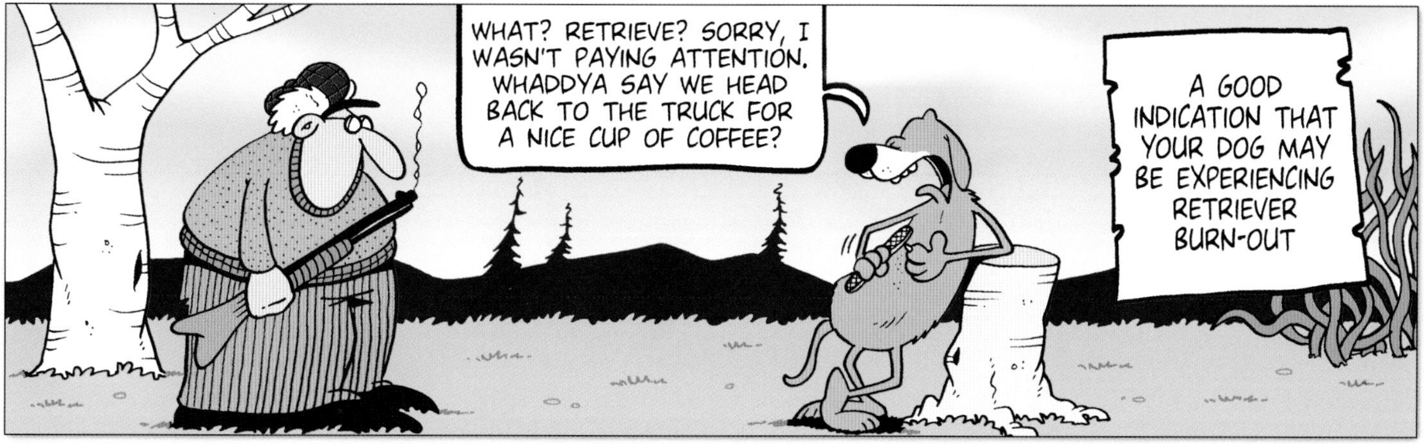
WHAT? RETRIEVE? SORRY, I WASN'T PAYING ATTENTION. WHADDYA SAY WE HEAD BACK TO THE TRUCK FOR A NICE CUP OF COFFEE?
A GOOD INDICATION THAT YOUR DOG MAY BE EXPERIENCING RETRIEVER BURN-OUT

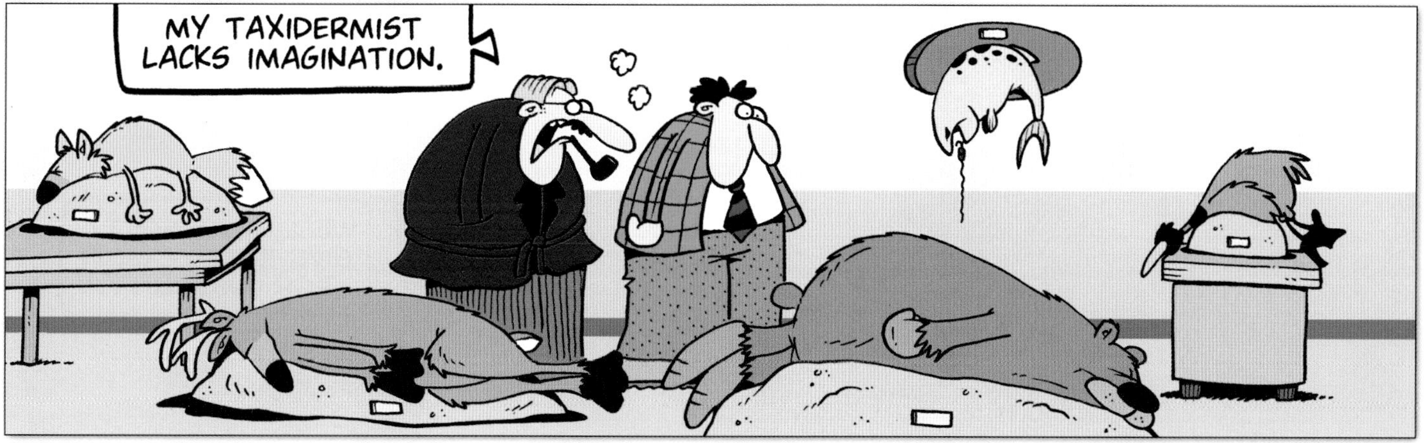
MY TAXIDERMIST LACKS IMAGINATION.

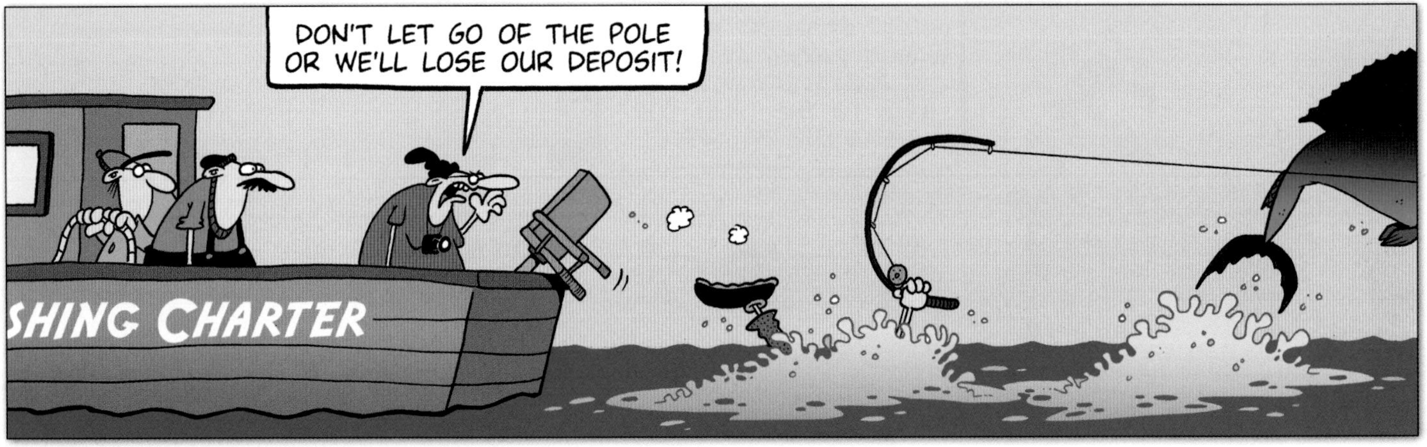
DON'T LET GO OF THE POLE OR WE'LL LOSE OUR DEPOSIT!
SHING CHARTER

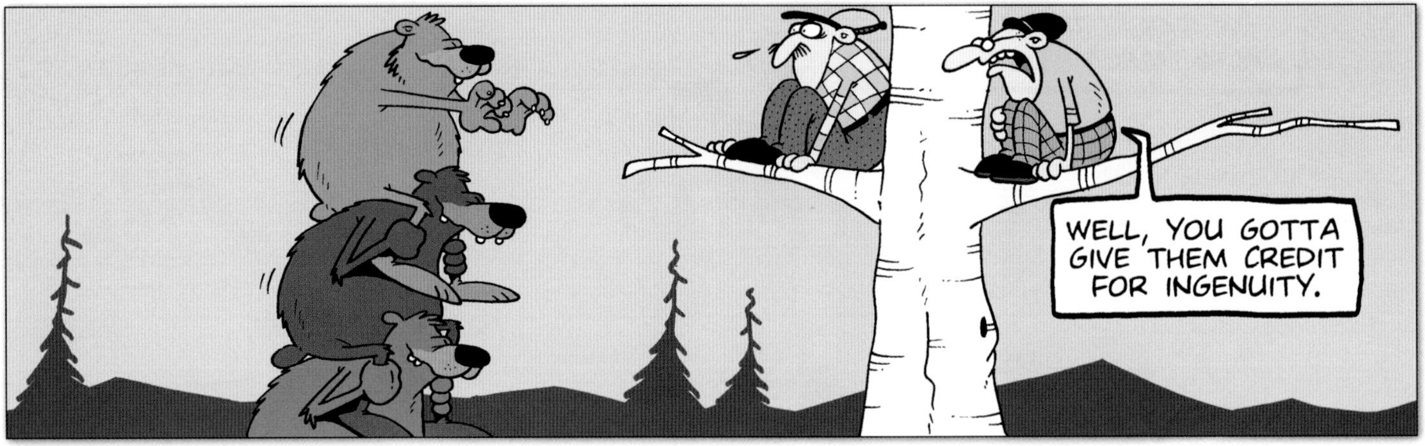
WELL, YOU GOTTA GIVE THEM CREDIT FOR INGENUITY.

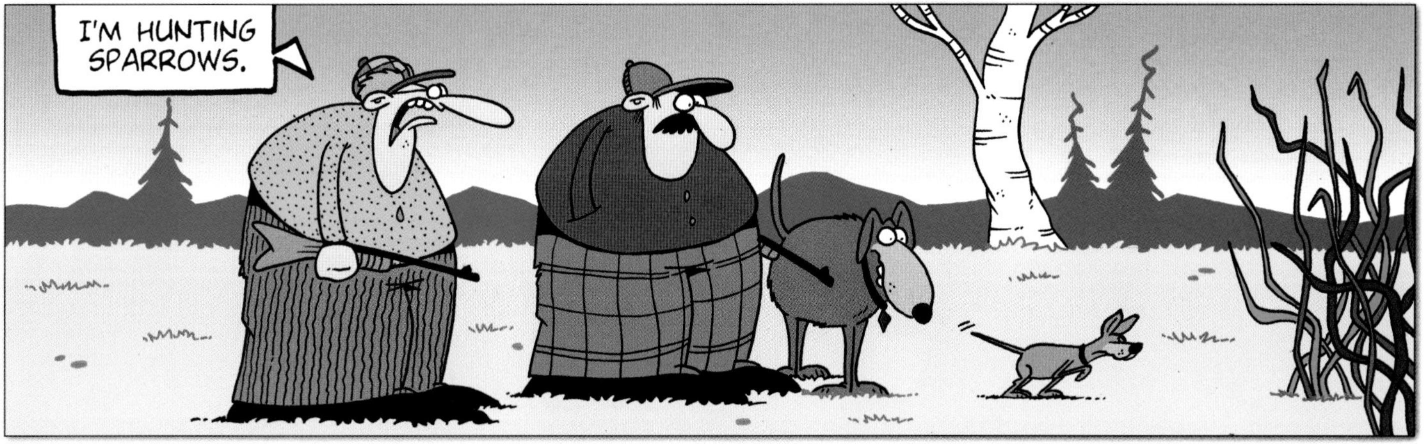
I'M HUNTING SPARROWS.

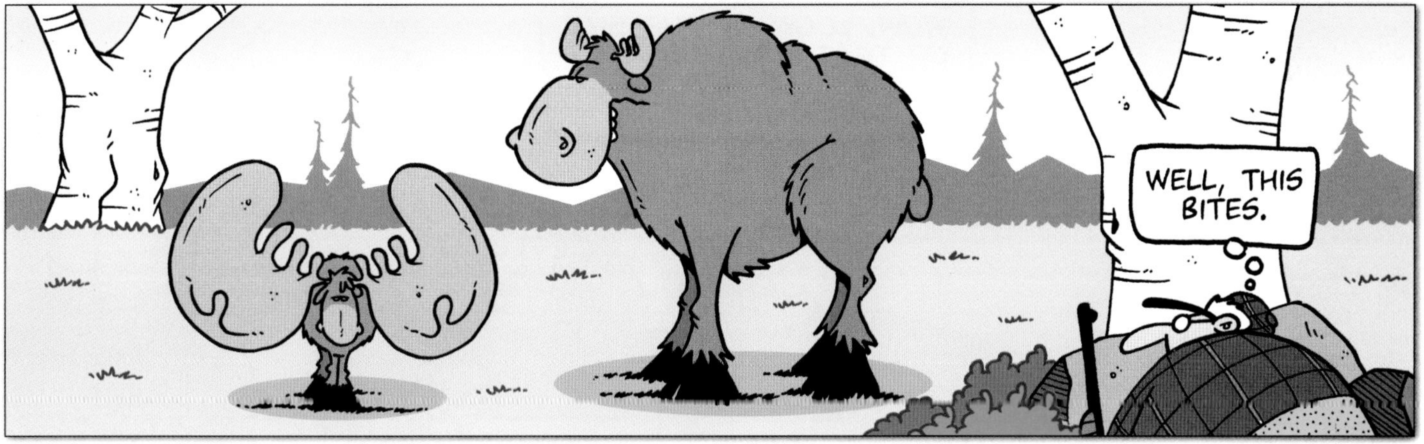
WELL, THIS BITES.

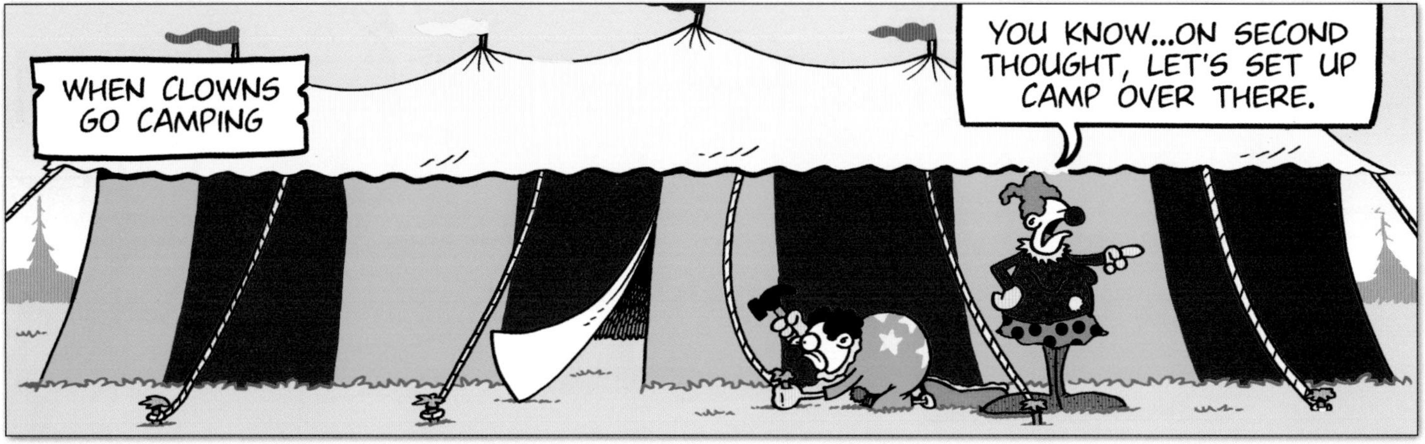
WHEN CLOWNS GO CAMPING
YOU KNOW...ON SECOND THOUGHT, LET'S SET UP CAMP OVER THERE.

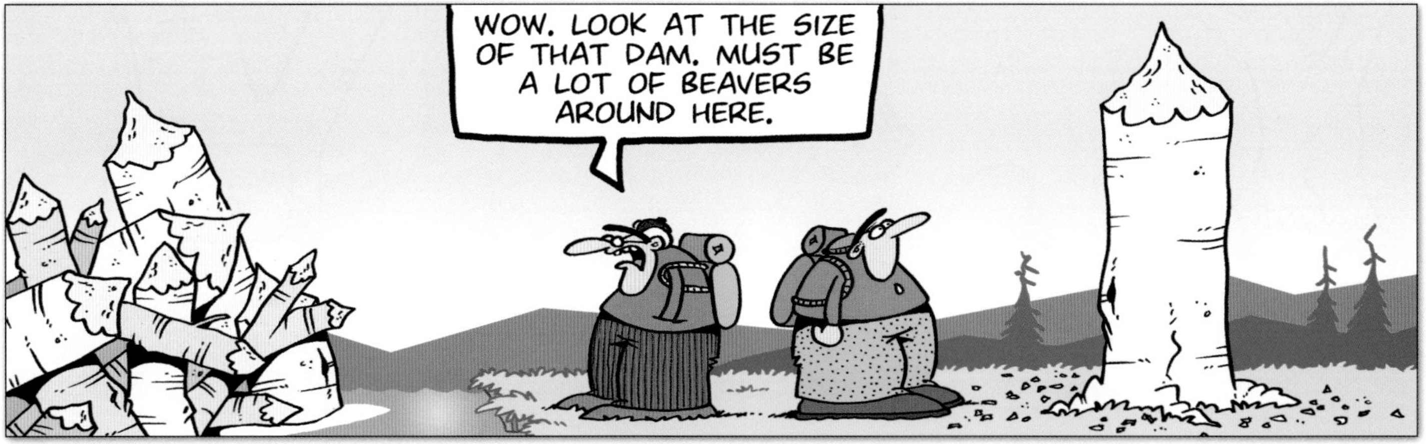
WOW. LOOK AT THE SIZE OF THAT DAM. MUST BE A LOT OF BEAVERS AROUND HERE.

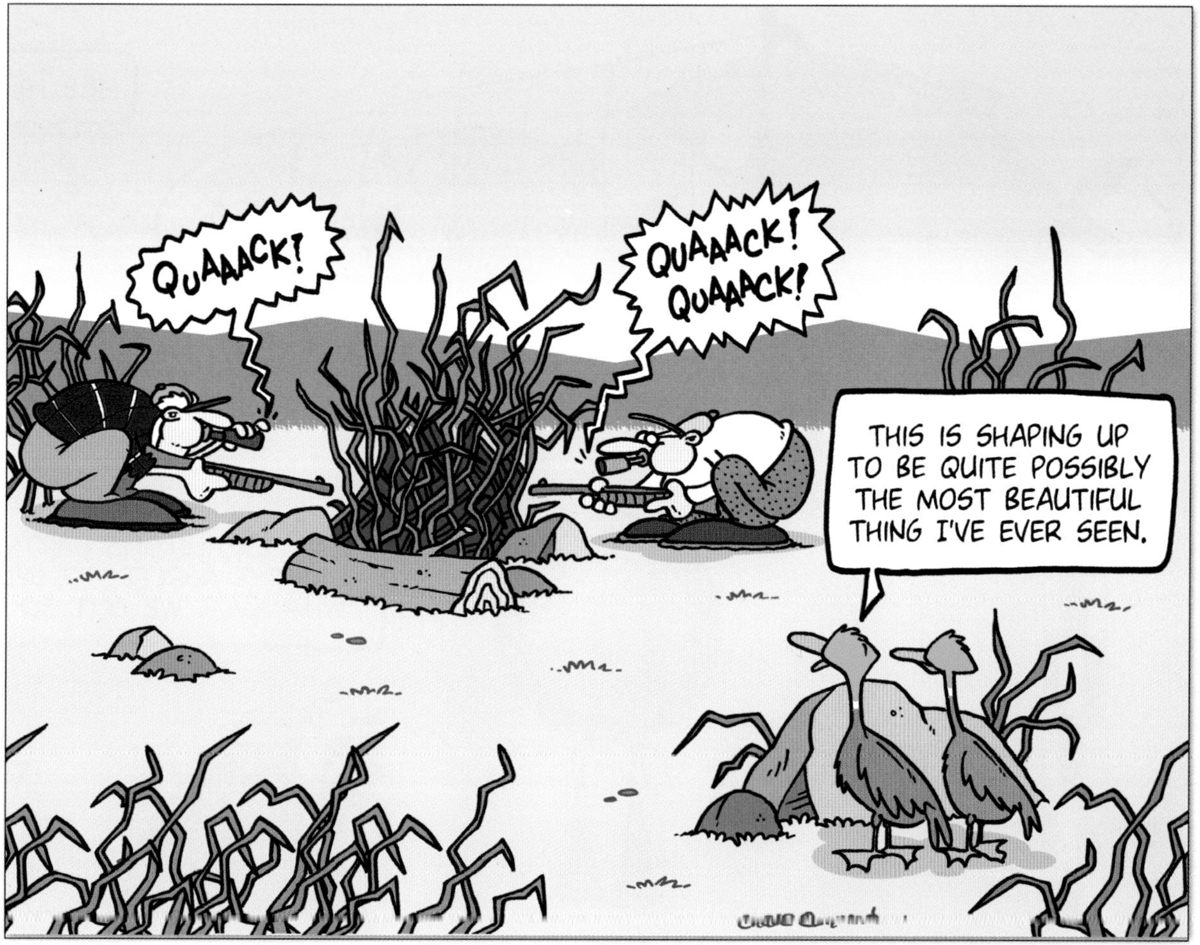
QUAAACK!
QUAAACK! QUAAACK!
THIS IS SHAPING UP TO BE QUITE POSSIBLY THE MOST BEAUTIFUL THING I'VE EVER SEEN.

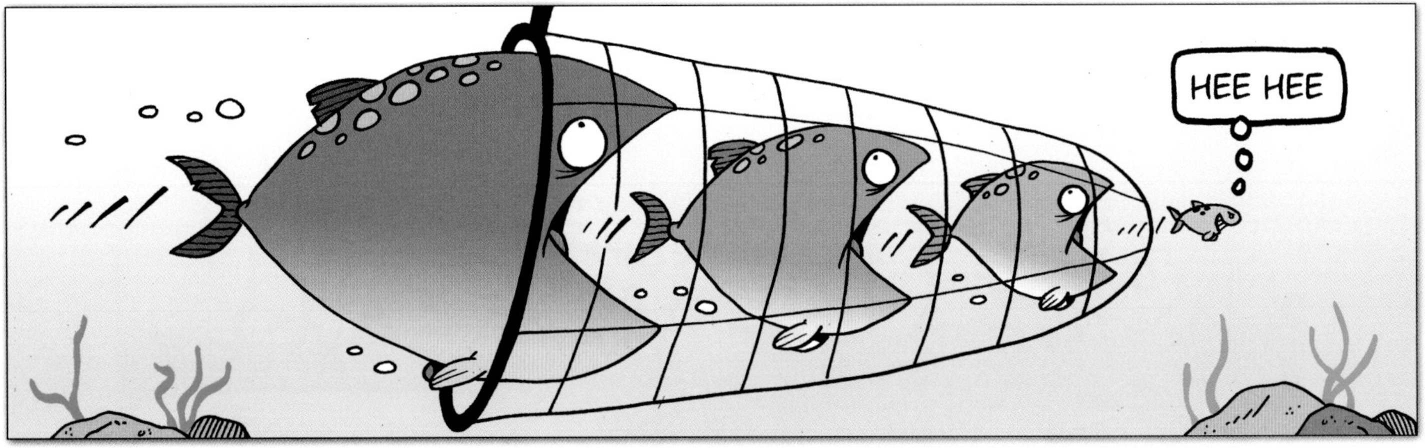
HEE HEE

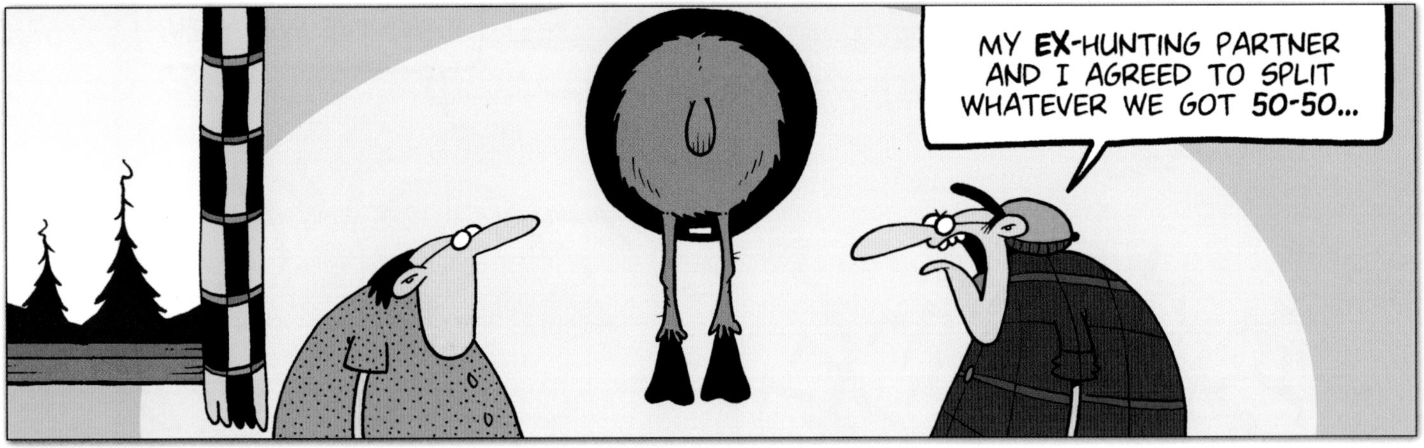
MY EX-HUNTING PARTNER AND I AGREED TO SPLIT WHATEVER WE GOT 50-50...

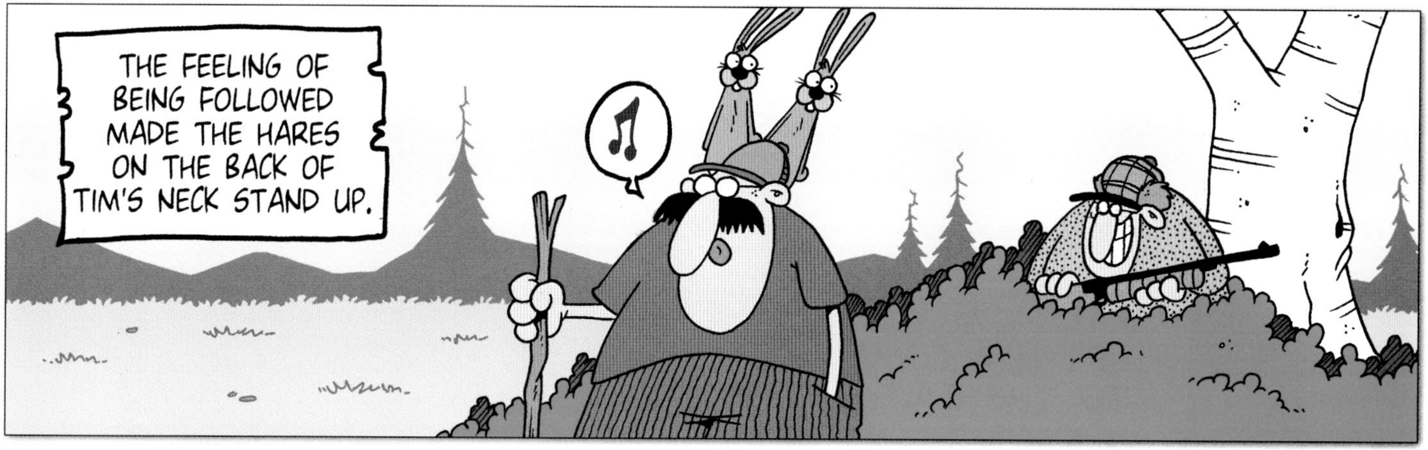
THE FEELING OF BEING FOLLOWED MADE THE HARES ON THE BACK OF TIM'S NECK STAND UP.

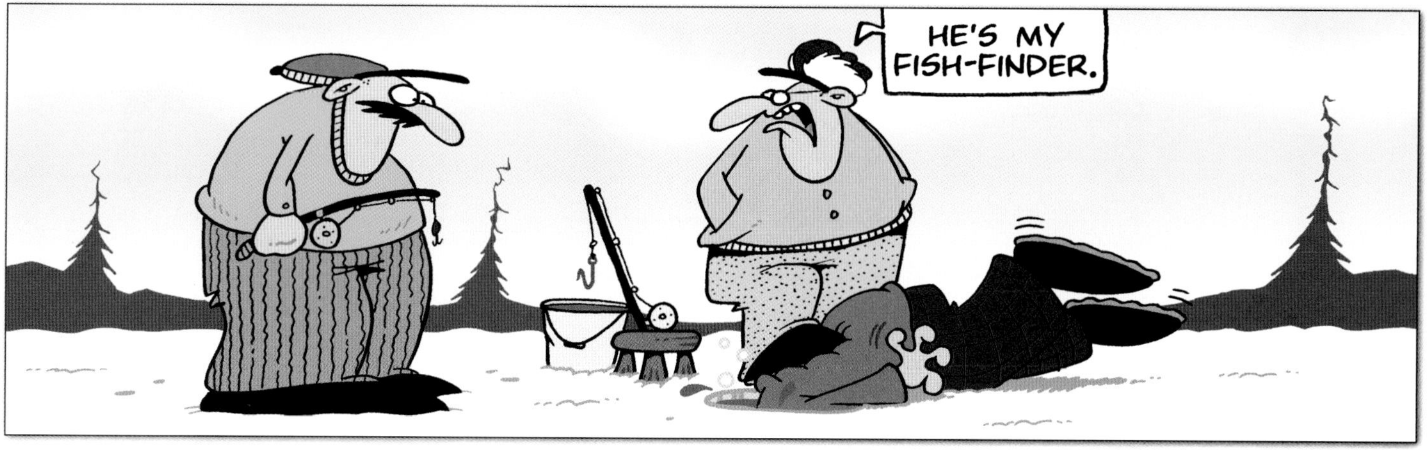
HE'S MY FISH-FINDER.

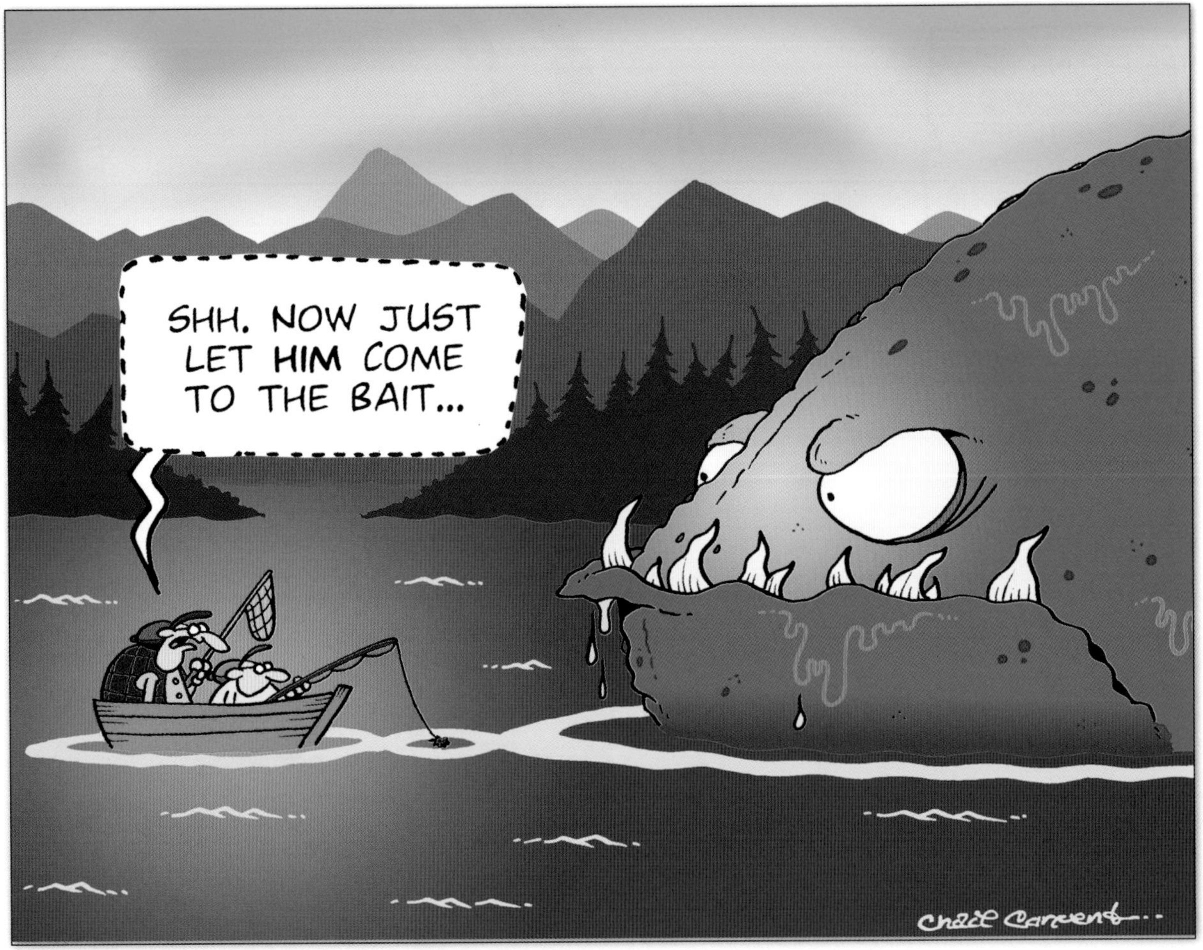
SHH. NOW JUST LET HIM COME TO THE BAIT...

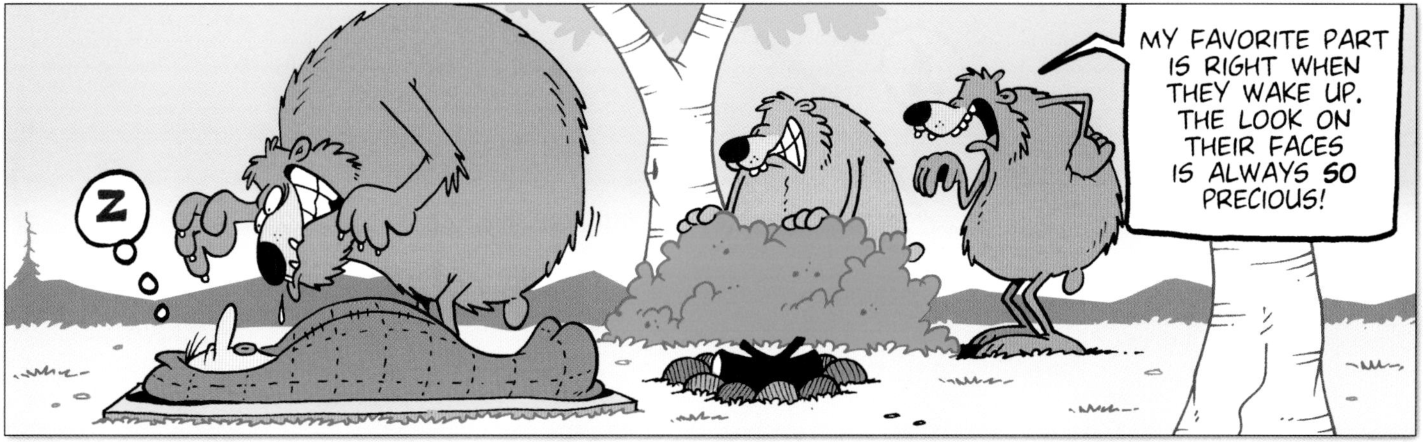
Z
MY FAVORITE PART IS RIGHT WHEN THEY WAKE UP. THE LOOK ON THEIR FACES IS ALWAYS SO PRECIOUS!

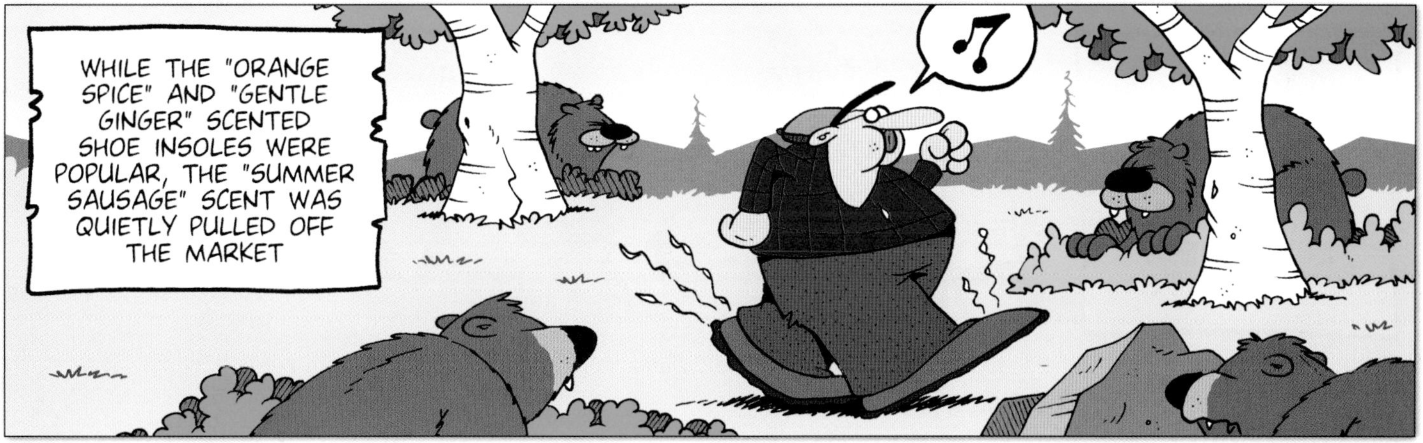
WHILE THE "ORANGE SPICE" AND "GENTLE GINGER" SCENTED SHOE INSOLES WERE POPULAR, THE "SUMMER SAUSAGE" SCENT WAS QUIETLY PULLED OFF THE MARKET

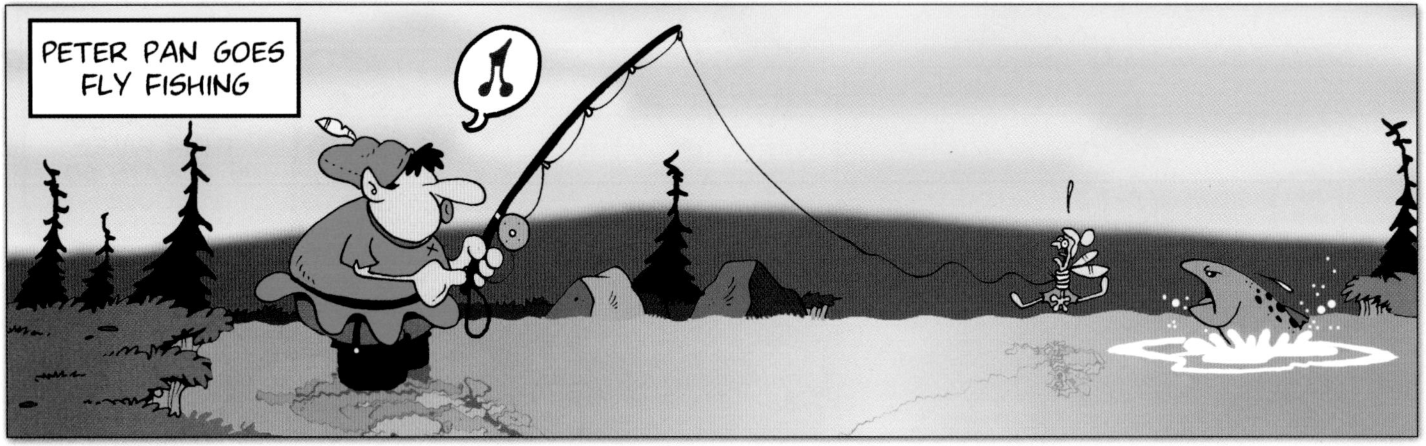
PETER PAN GOES FLY FISHING

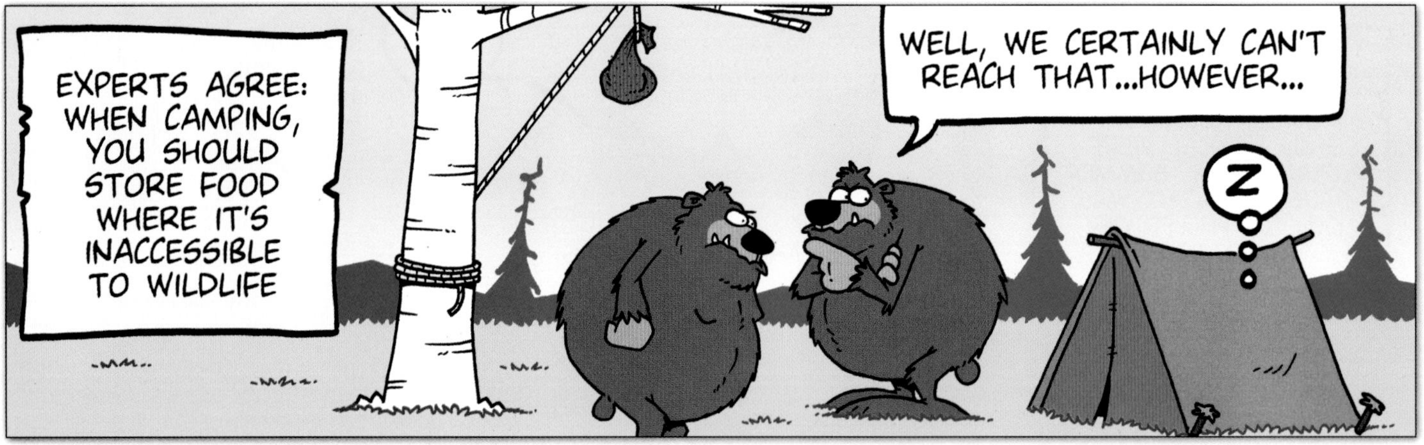
EXPERTS AGREE: WHEN CAMPING, YOU SHOULD STORE FOOD WHERE IT'S INACCESSIBLE TO WILDLIFE
WELL, WE CERTAINLY CAN'T REACH THAT...HOWEVER...
Z

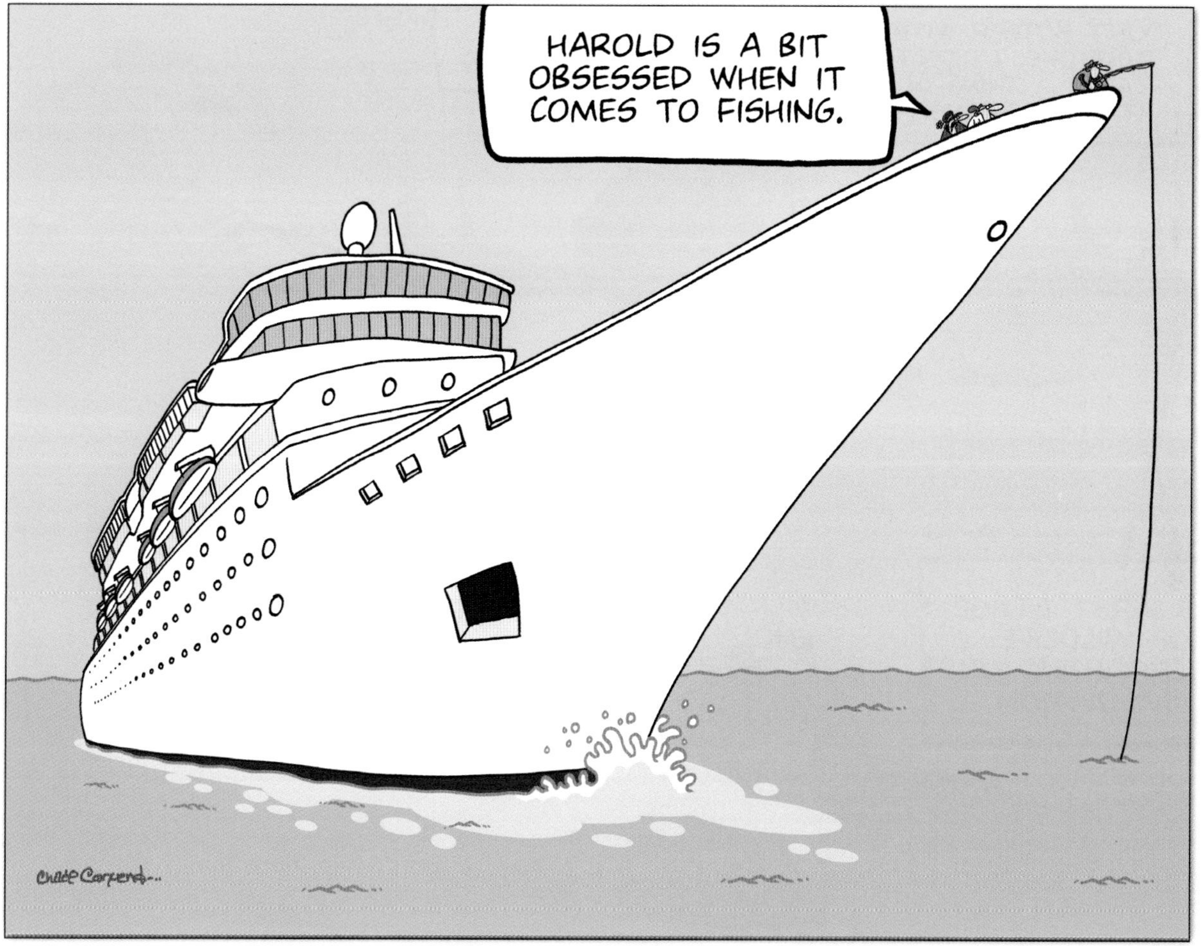
HAROLD IS A BIT OBSESSED WHEN IT COMES TO FISHING.

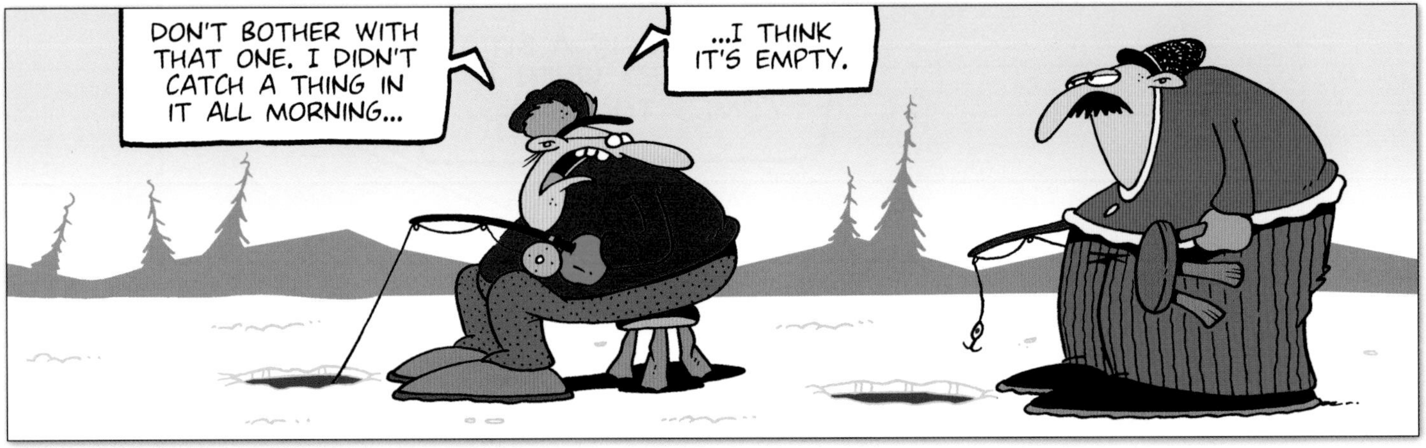
DON'T BOTHER WITH THAT ONE. I DIDN'T CATCH A THING IN IT ALL MORNING...
...I THINK IT'S EMPTY.

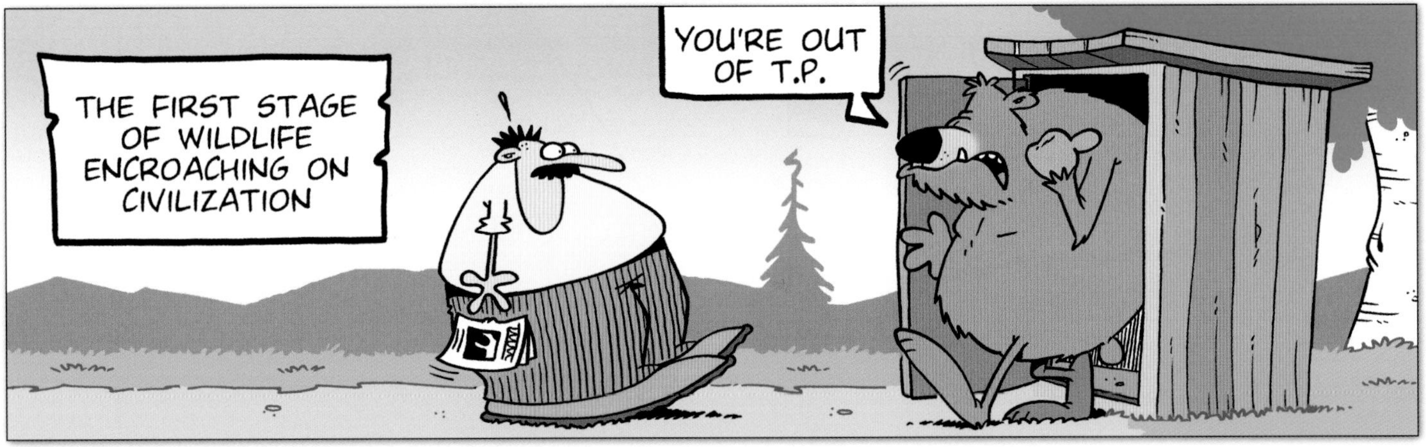
THE FIRST STAGE OF WILDLIFE ENCROACHING ON CIVILIZATION
YOU'RE OUT OF T.P.

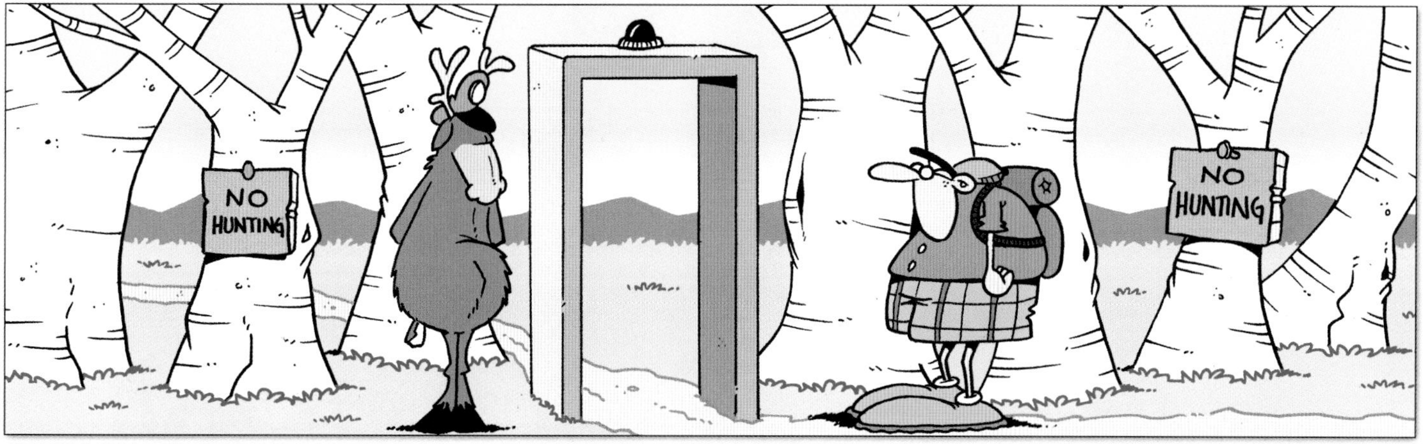
NO HUNTING
NO HUNTING

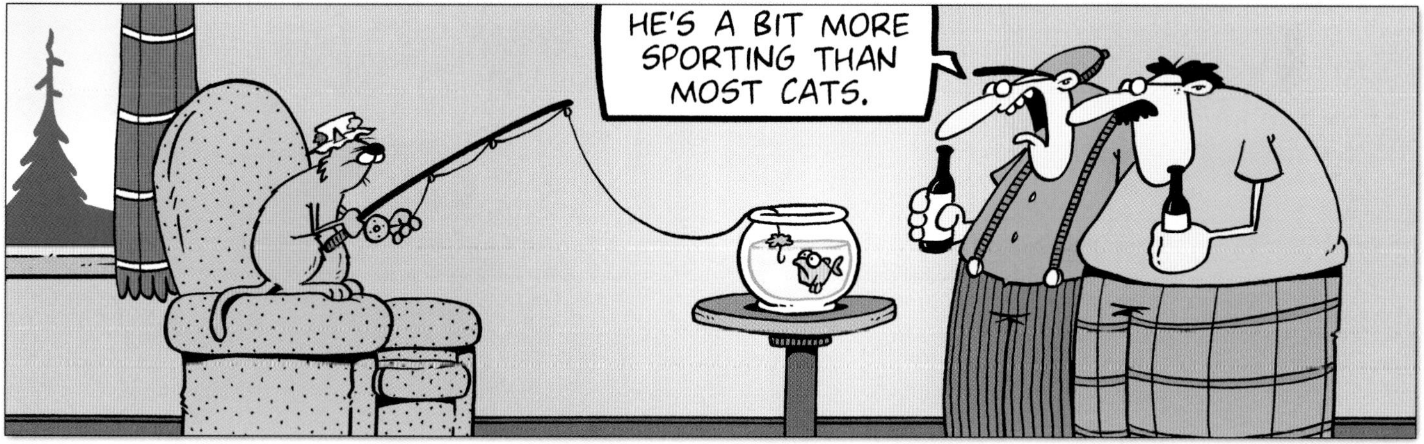
HE'S A BIT MORE SPORTING THAN MOST CATS.

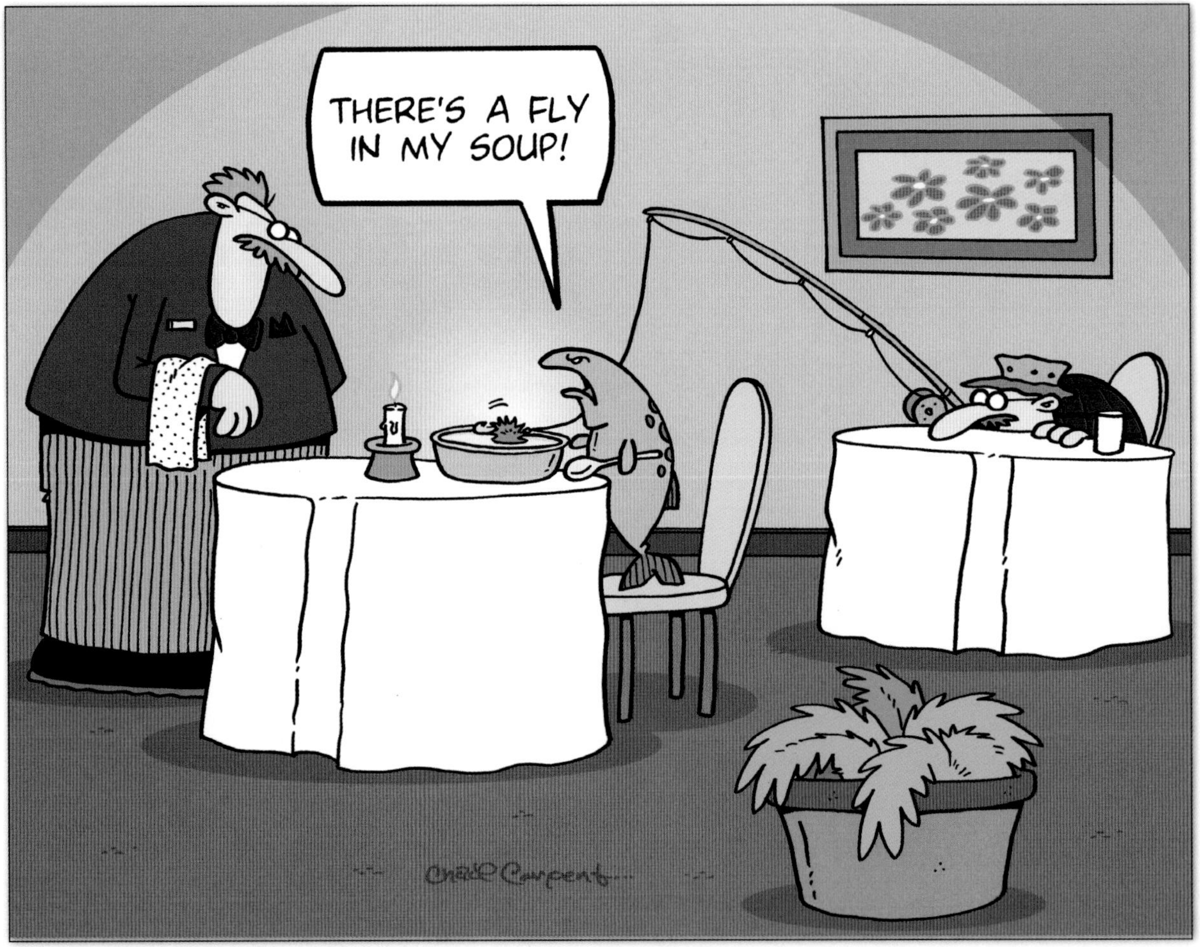
THERE'S A FLY IN MY SOUP!

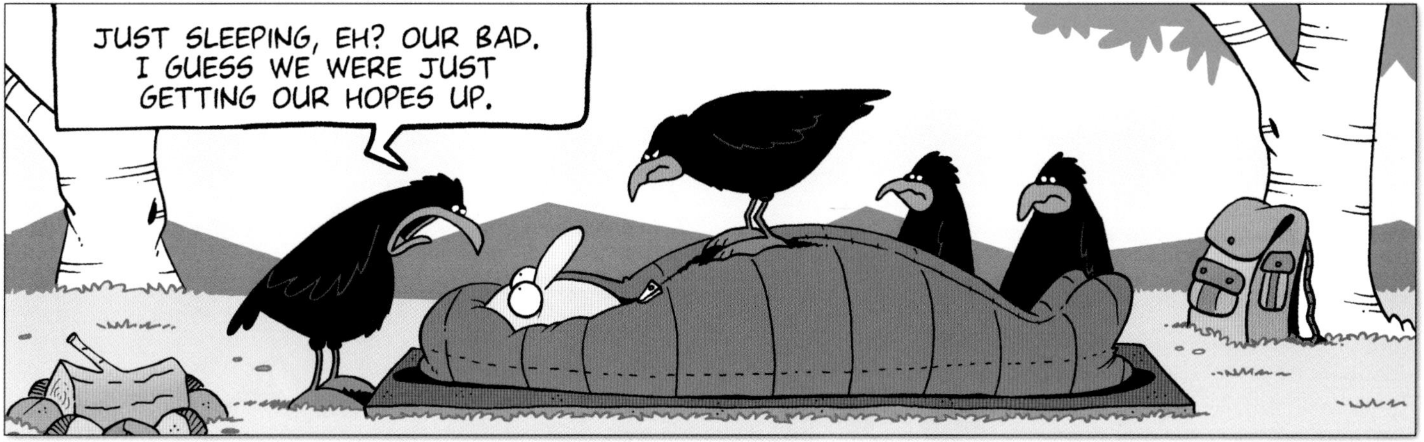
JUST SLEEPING, EH? OUR BAD. I GUESS WE WERE JUST GETTING OUR HOPES UP.

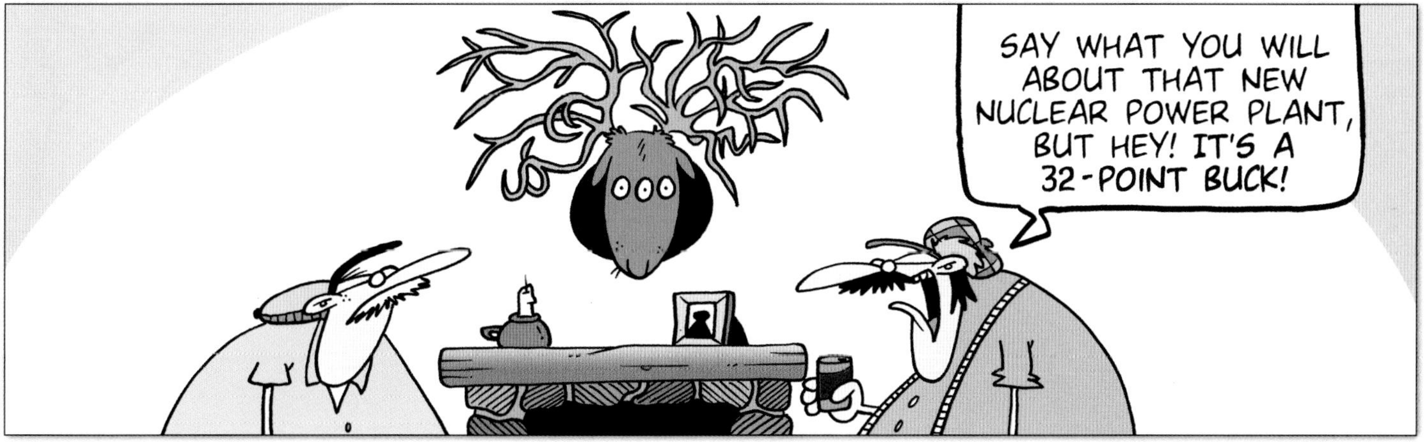
SAY WHAT YOU WILL ABOUT THAT NEW NUCLEAR POWER PLANT, BUT HEY! IT'S A 32-POINT BUCK!

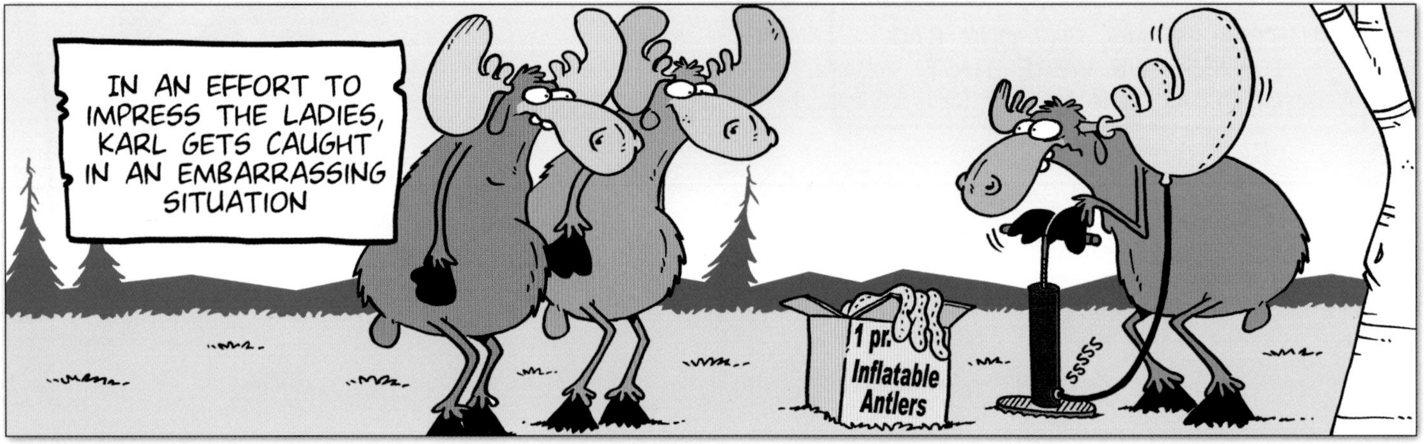
IN AN EFFORT TO IMPRESS THE LADIES, KARL GETS CAUGHT IN AN EMBARRASSING SITUATION
1 pr. Inflatable Antlers
SSSSS

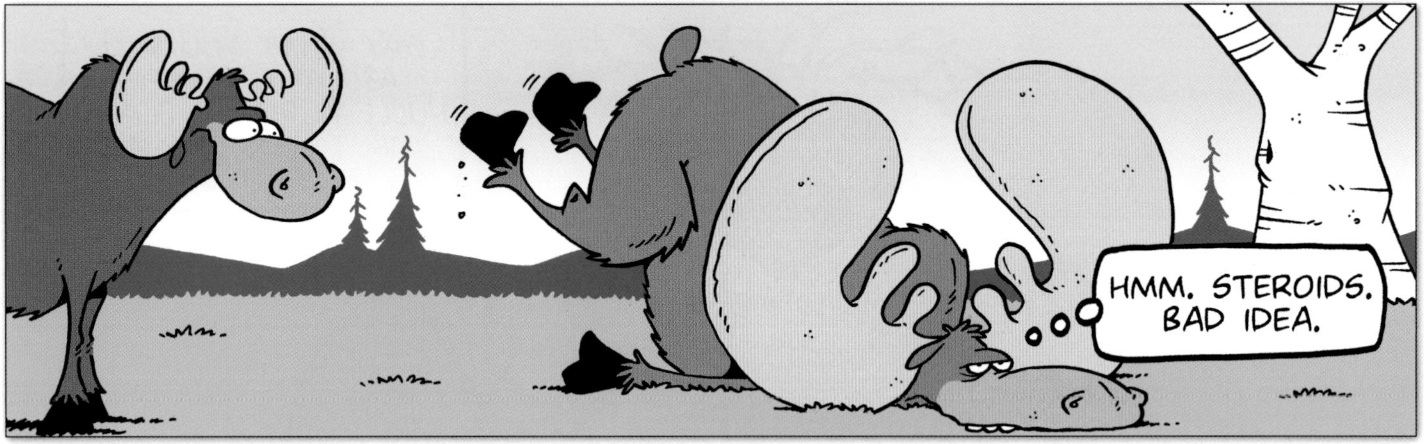
HMM. STEROIDS. BAD IDEA.

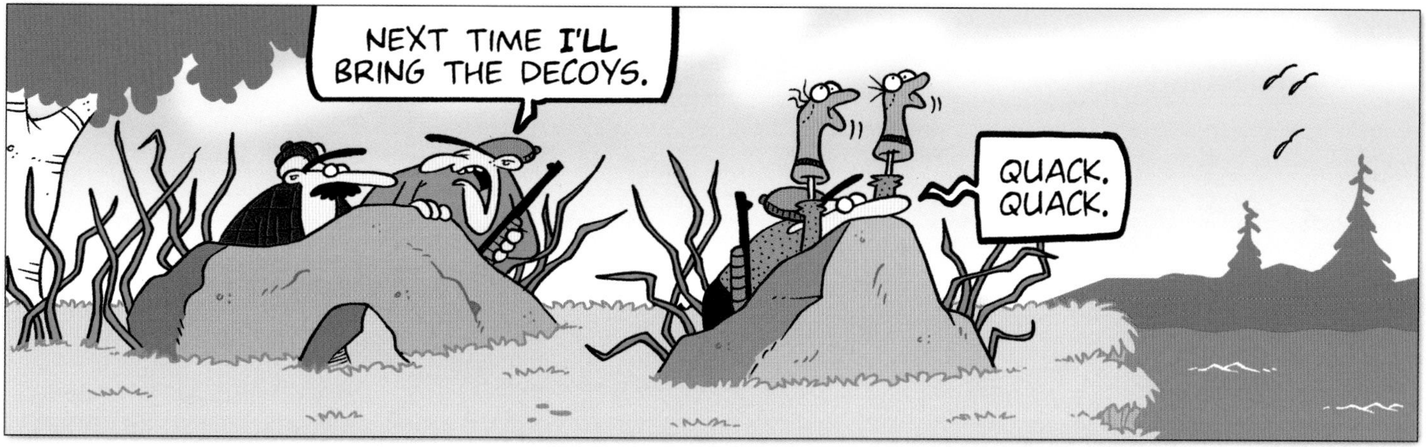
NEXT TIME I'LL BRING THE DECOYS.
QUACK. QUACK.

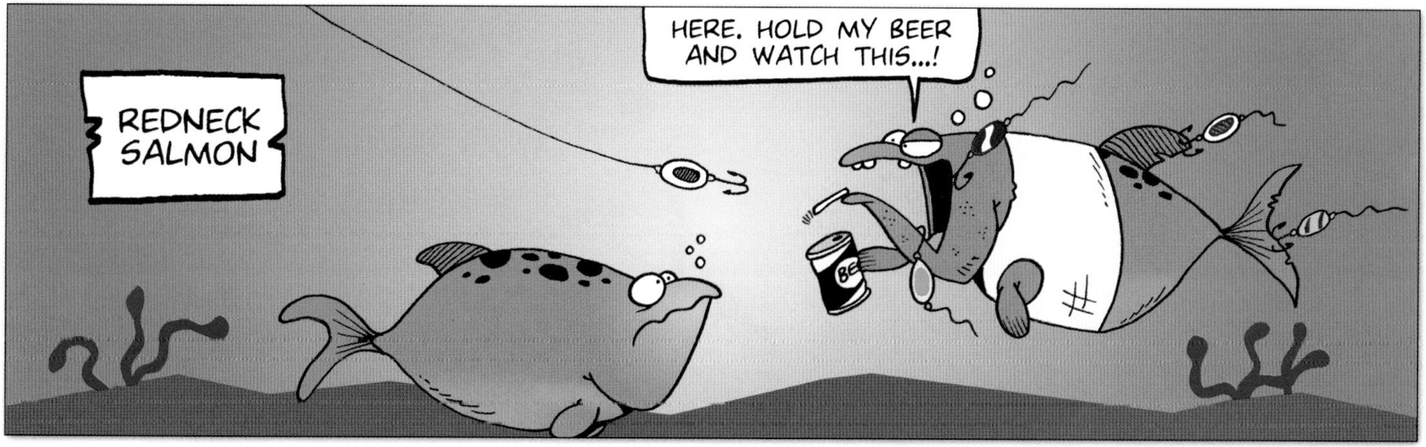
REDNECK SALMON
HERE. HOLD MY BEER AND WATCH THIS...!

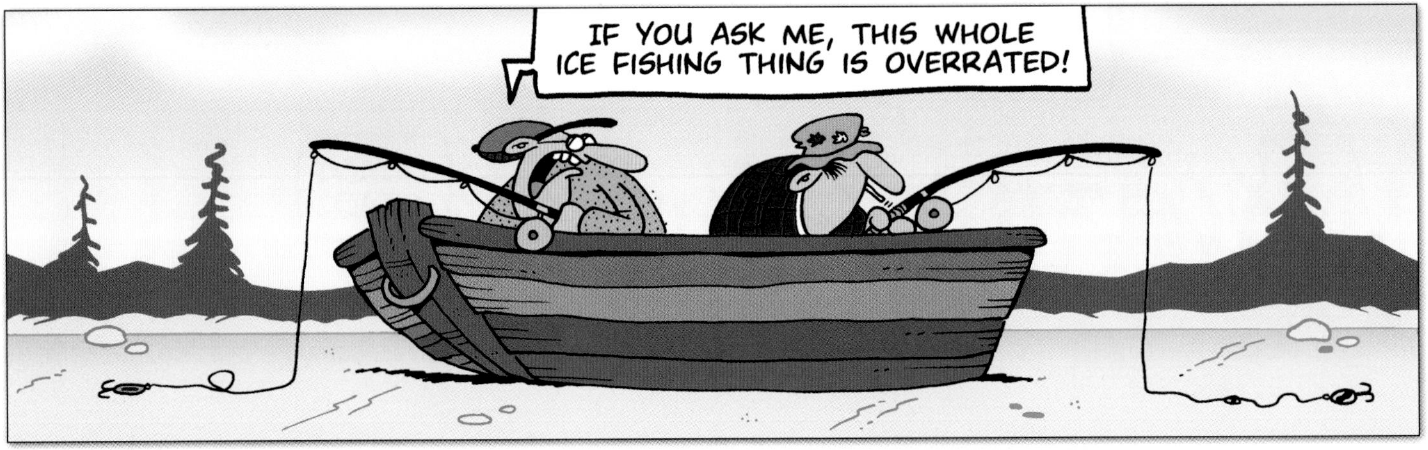
IF YOU ASK ME, THIS WHOLE ICE FISHING THING IS OVERRATED!

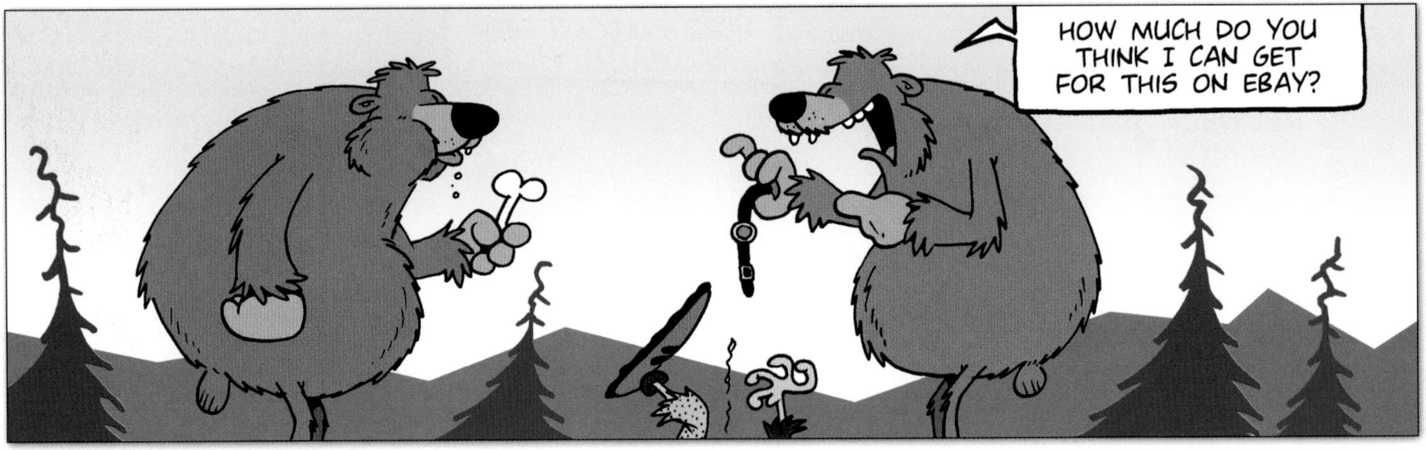
HOW MUCH DO YOU THINK I CAN GET FOR THIS ON EBAY?

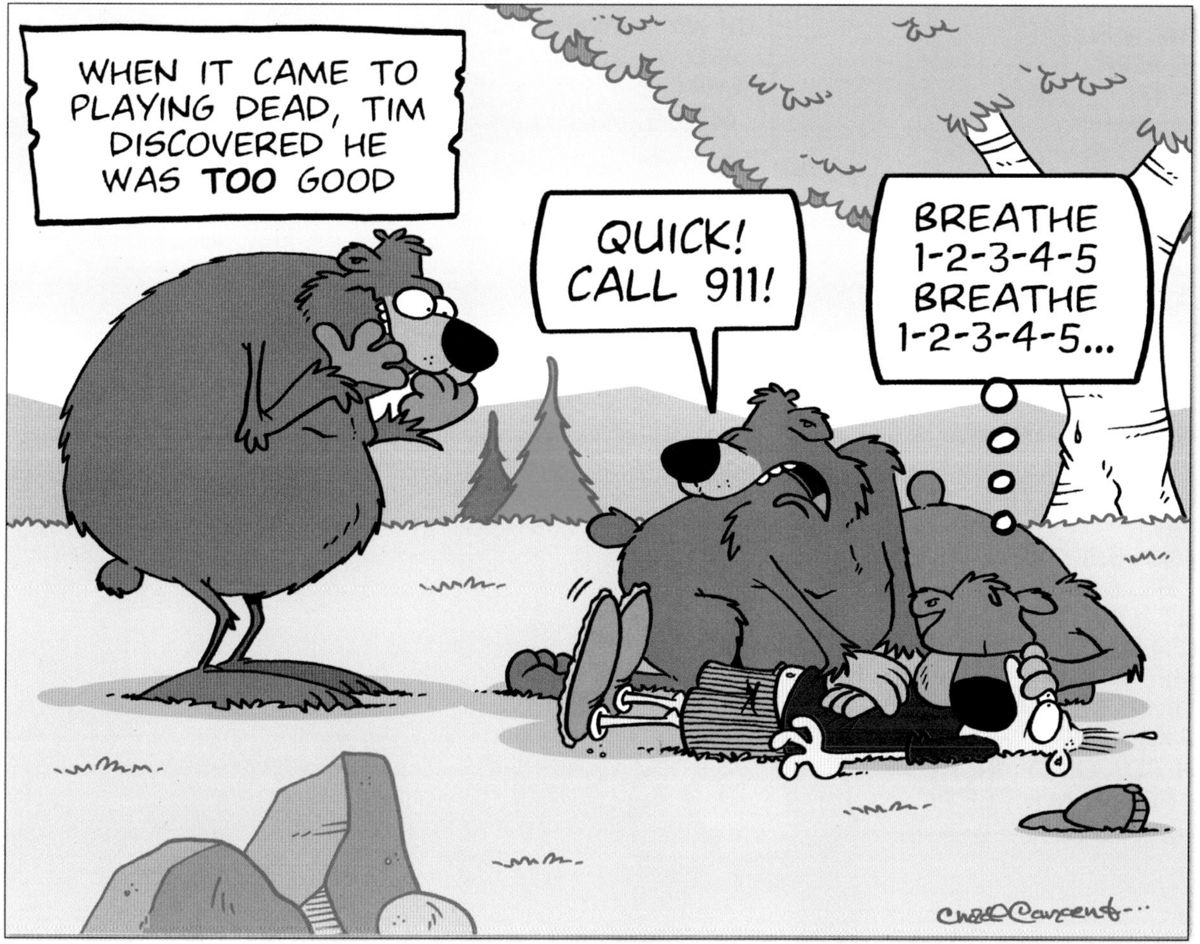
WHEN IT CAME TO PLAYING DEAD, TIM DISCOVERED HE WAS **TOO** GOOD
QUICK! CALL 911!
BREATHE 1-2-3-4-5 BREATHE 1-2-3-4-5...

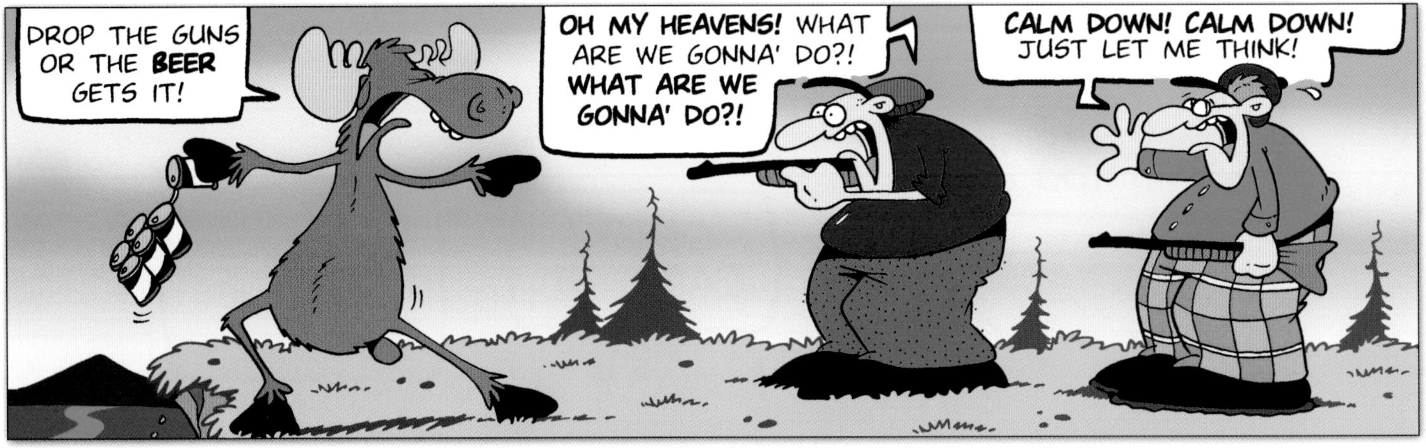
DROP THE GUNS OR THE BEER GETS IT!
OH MY HEAVENS! WHAT ARE WE GONNA' DO?! WHAT ARE WE GONNA' DO?!
CALM DOWN! CALM DOWN! JUST LET ME THINK!

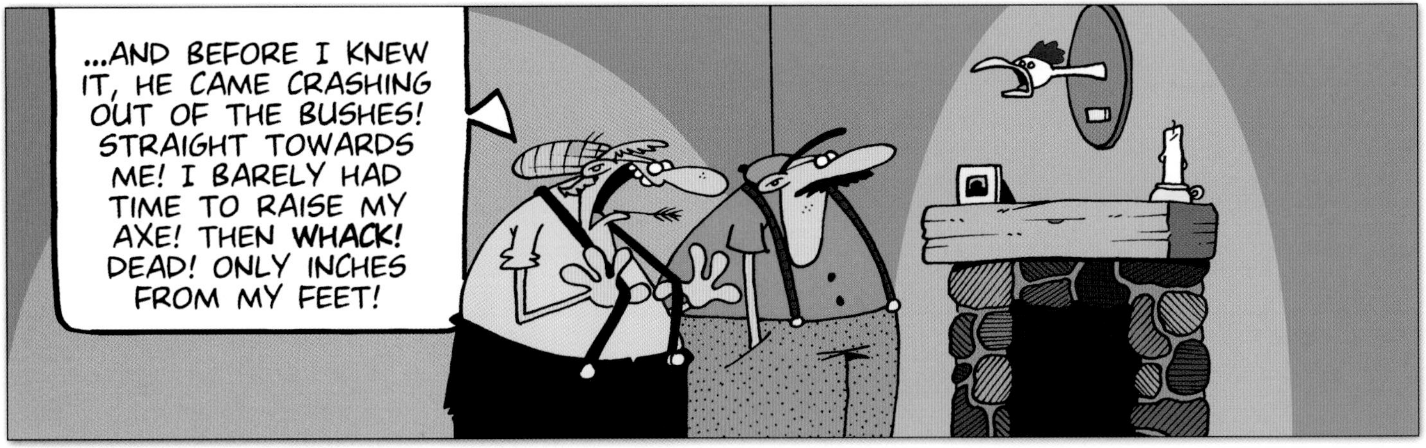
...AND BEFORE I KNEW IT, HE CAME CRASHING OUT OF THE BUSHES! STRAIGHT TOWARDS ME! I BARELY HAD TIME TO RAISE MY AXE! THEN WHACK! DEAD! ONLY INCHES FROM MY FEET!

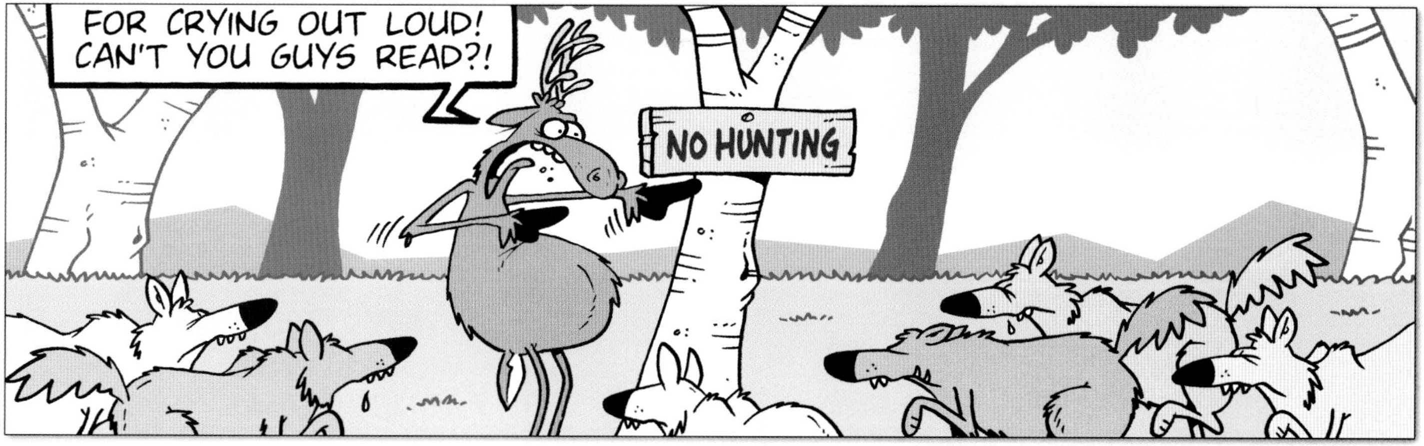
FOR CRYING OUT LOUD! CAN'T YOU GUYS READ?!
NO HUNTING

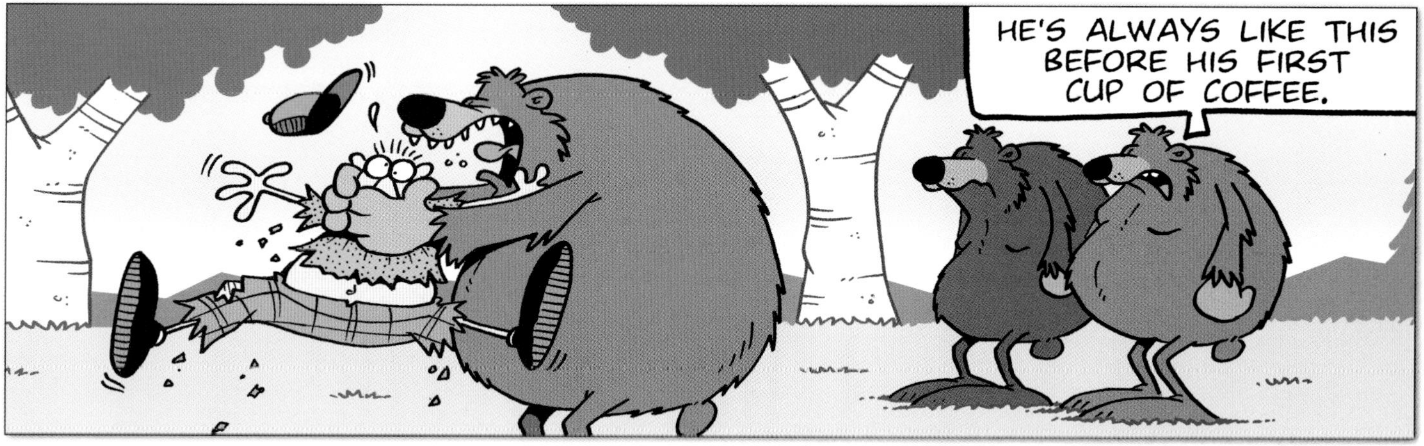
HE'S ALWAYS LIKE THIS BEFORE HIS FIRST CUP OF COFFEE.

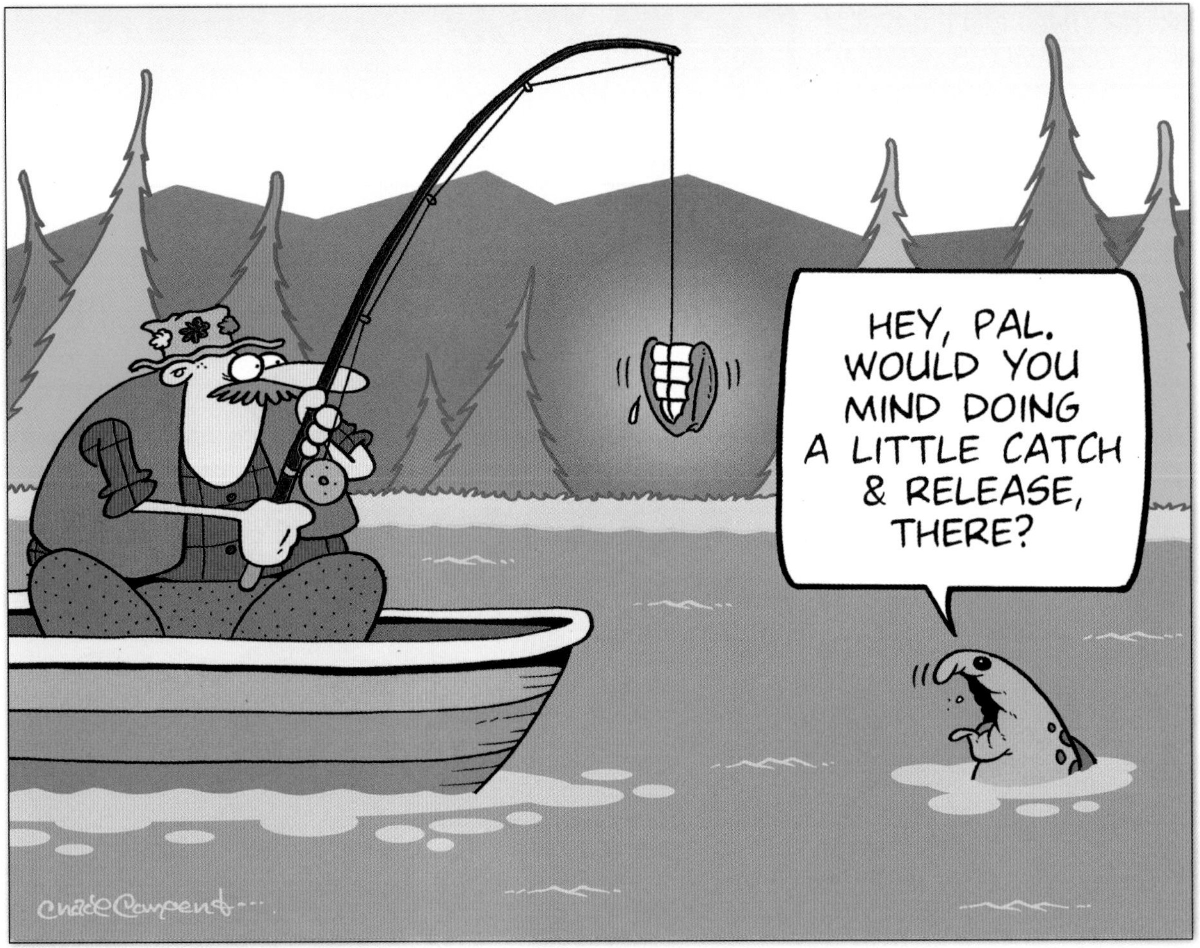
HEY, PAL. WOULD YOU MIND DOING A LITTLE CATCH & RELEASE, THERE?

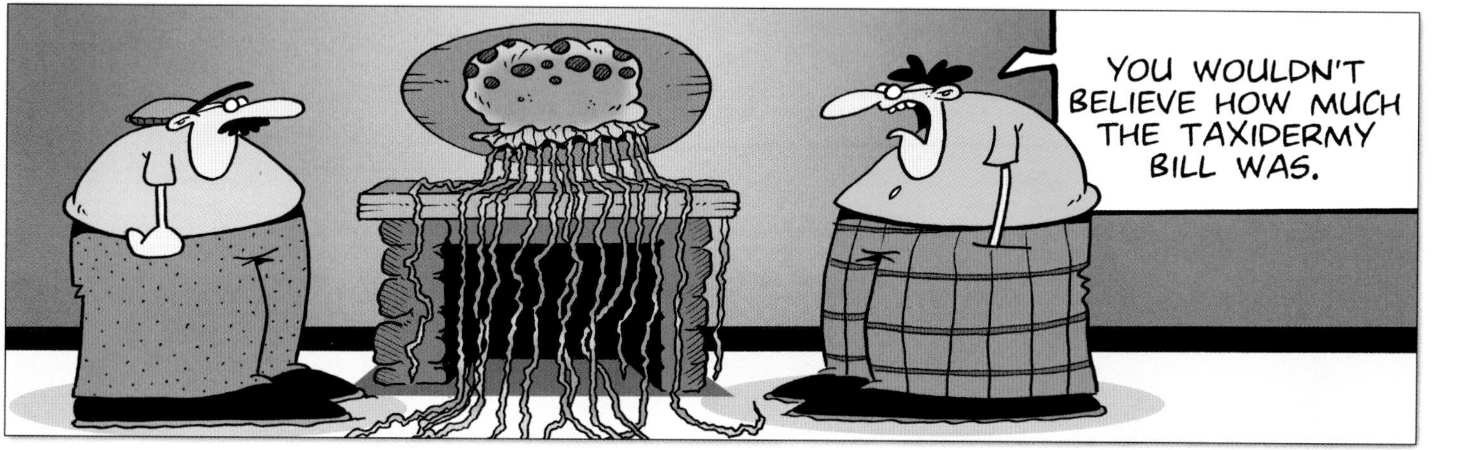
YOU WOULDN'T BELIEVE HOW MUCH THE TAXIDERMY BILL WAS.

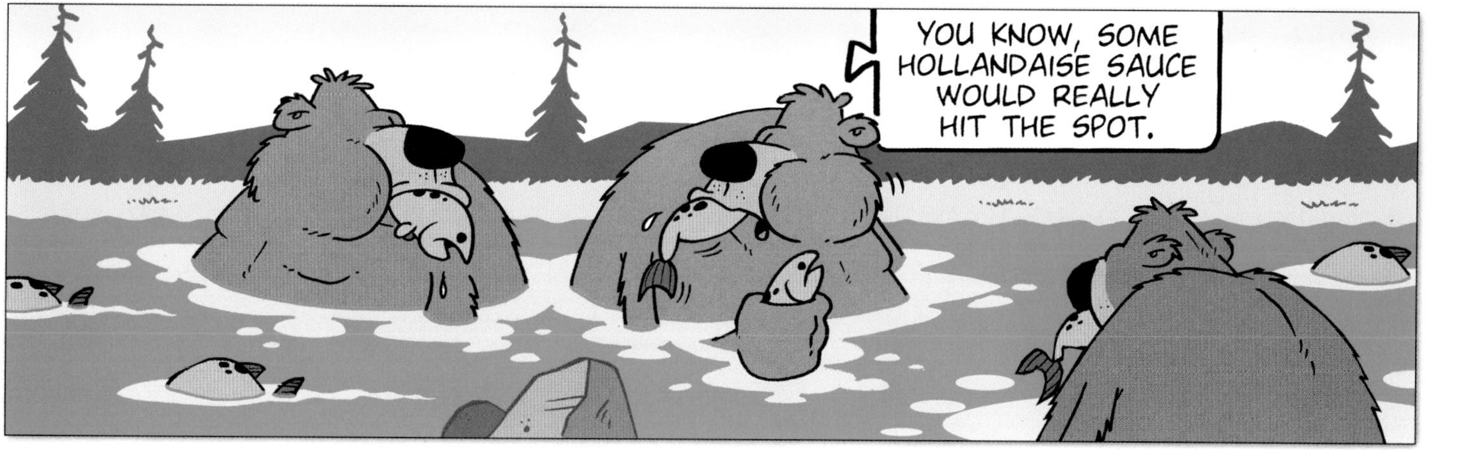
YOU KNOW, SOME HOLLANDAISE SAUCE WOULD REALLY HIT THE SPOT.

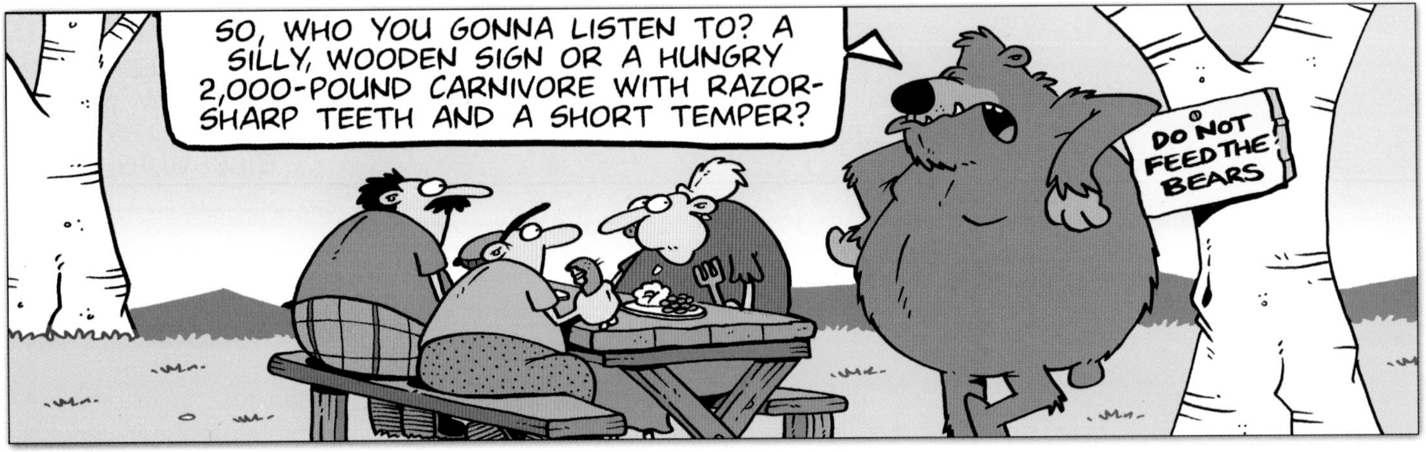
SO, WHO YOU GONNA LISTEN TO? A SILLY, WOODEN SIGN OR A HUNGRY 2,000-POUND CARNIVORE WITH RAZOR-SHARP TEETH AND A SHORT TEMPER?
DO NOT FEED THE BEARS

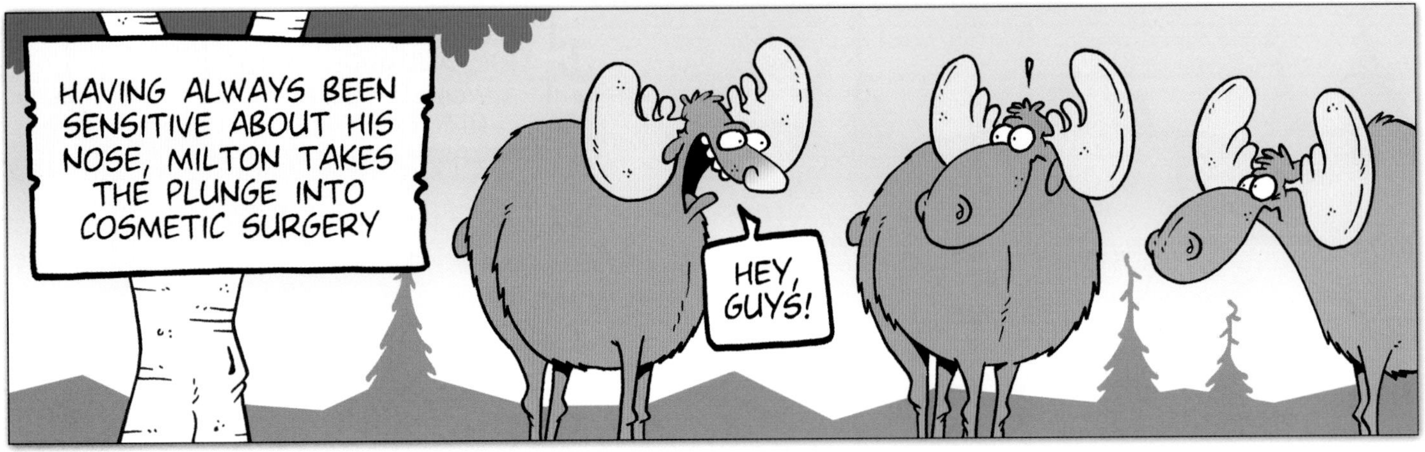
HAVING ALWAYS BEEN SENSITIVE ABOUT HIS NOSE, MILTON TAKES THE PLUNGE INTO COSMETIC SURGERY
HEY, GUYS!
!

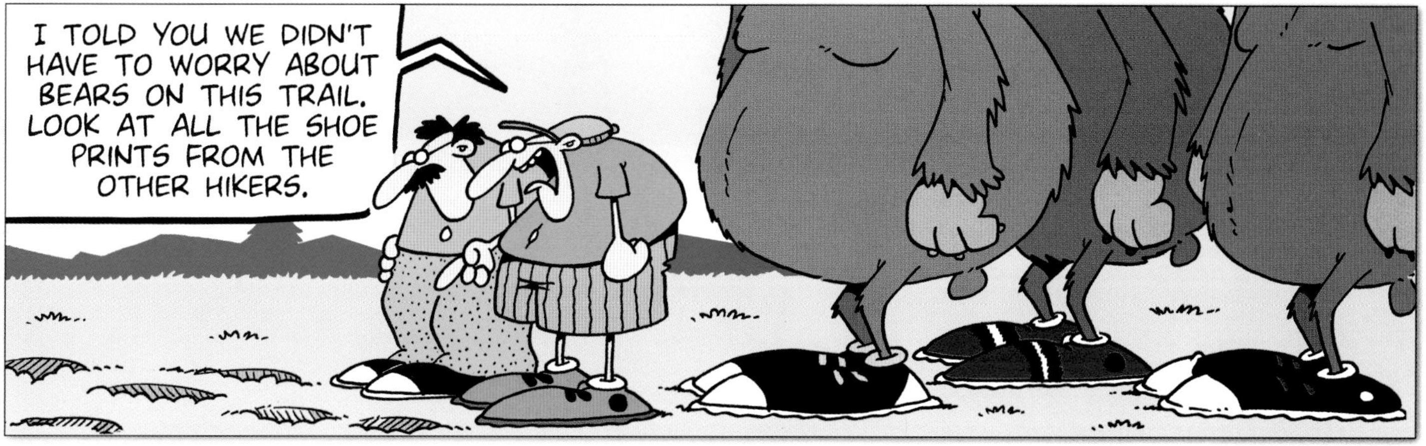
I TOLD YOU WE DIDN'T HAVE TO WORRY ABOUT BEARS ON THIS TRAIL. LOOK AT ALL THE SHOE PRINTS FROM THE OTHER HIKERS.

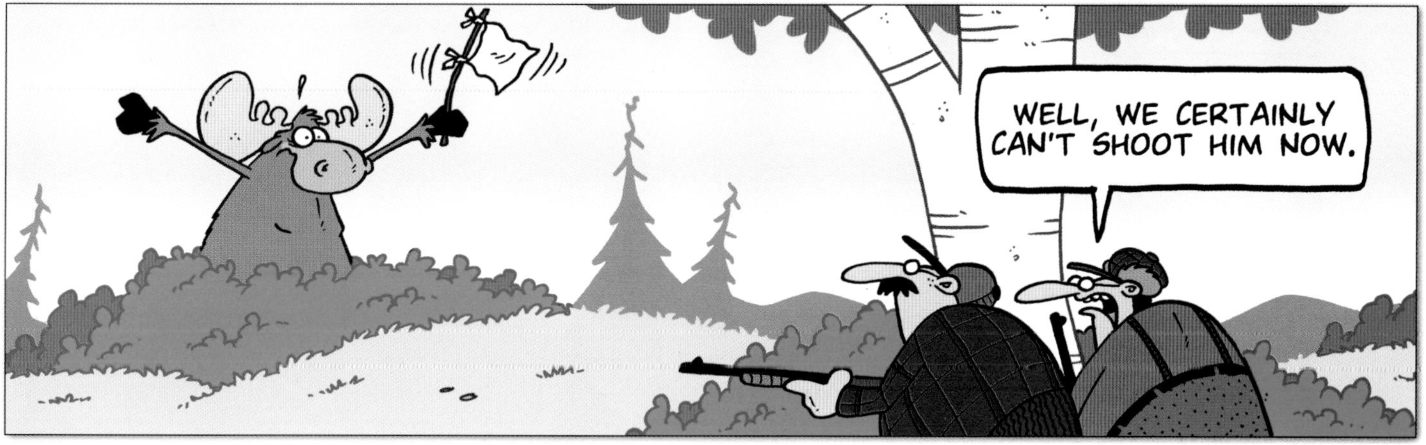
WELL, WE CERTAINLY CAN'T SHOOT HIM NOW.

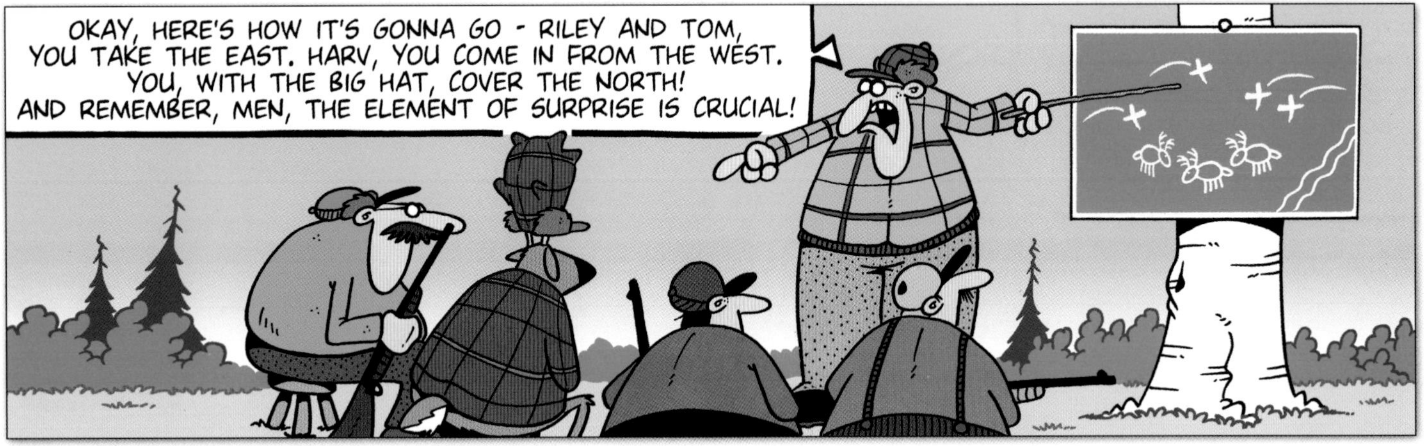
OKAY, HERE'S HOW IT'S GONNA GO - RILEY AND TOM, YOU TAKE THE EAST. HARV, YOU COME IN FROM THE WEST. YOU, WITH THE BIG HAT, COVER THE NORTH! AND REMEMBER, MEN, THE ELEMENT OF SURPRISE IS CRUCIAL!

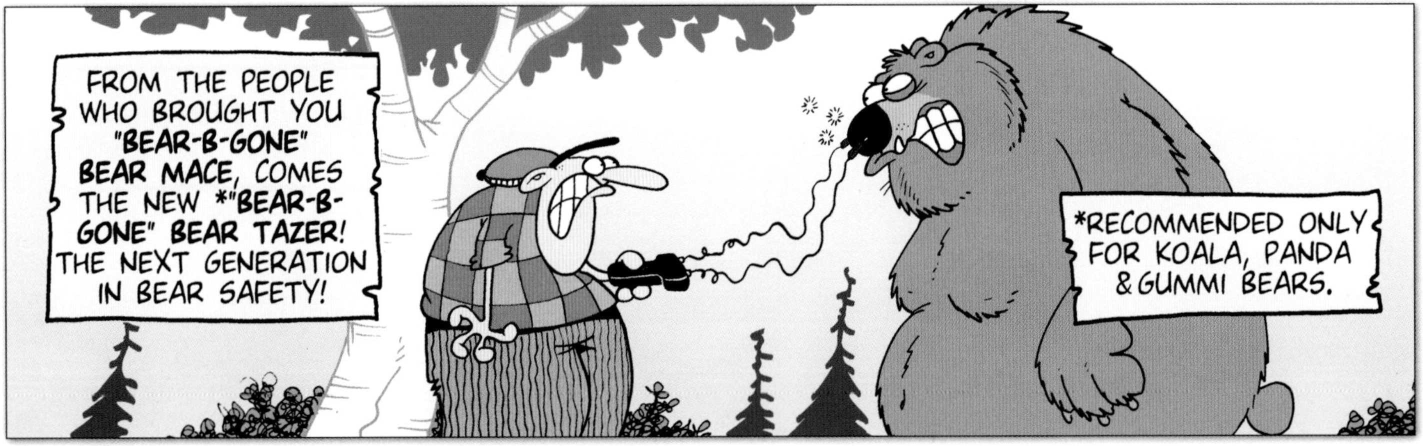
FROM THE PEOPLE WHO BROUGHT YOU "BEAR-B-GONE" BEAR MACE, COMES THE NEW *"BEAR-B-GONE" BEAR TAZER! THE NEXT GENERATION IN BEAR SAFETY!
*RECOMMENDED ONLY FOR KOALA, PANDA & GUMMI BEARS.

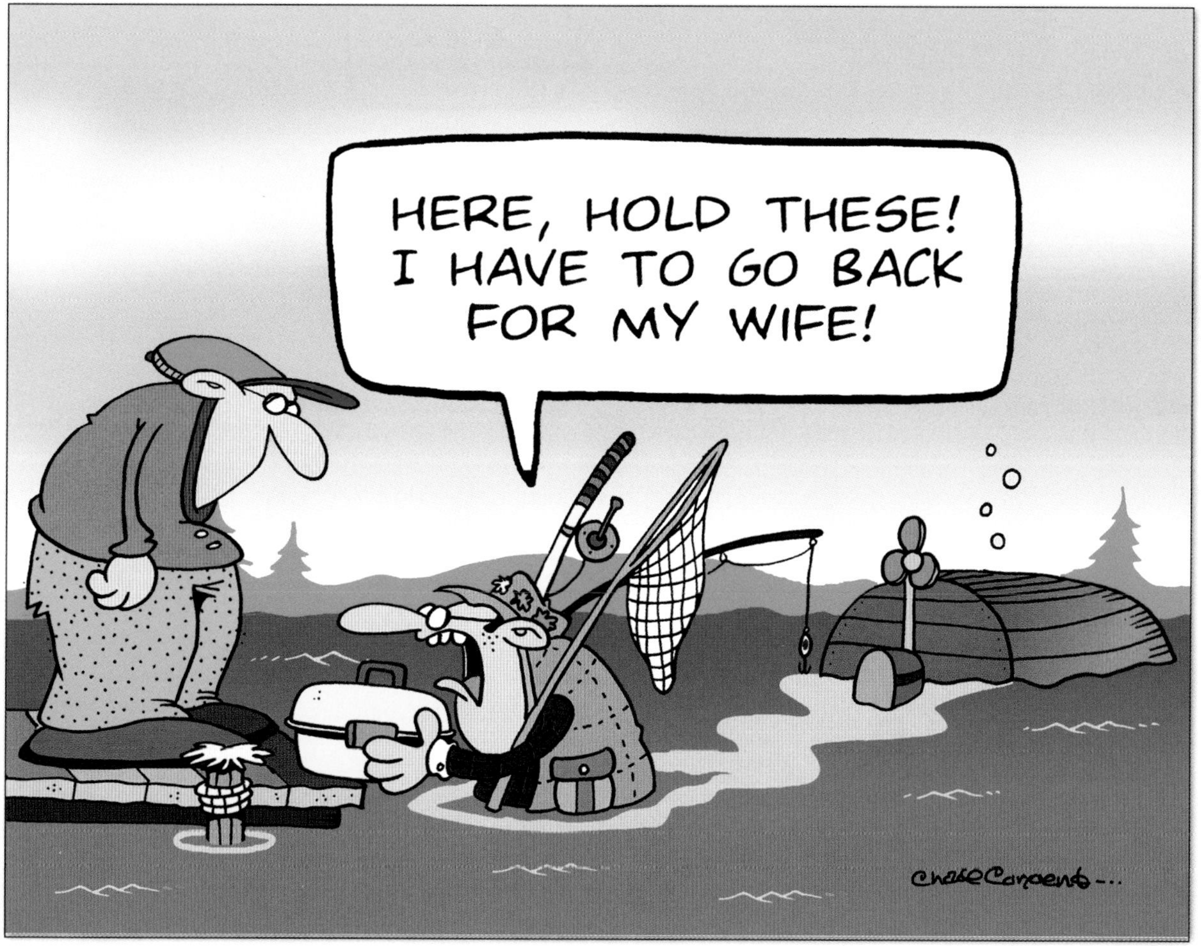
HERE, HOLD THESE! I HAVE TO GO BACK FOR MY WIFE!
chaseCarpenter...

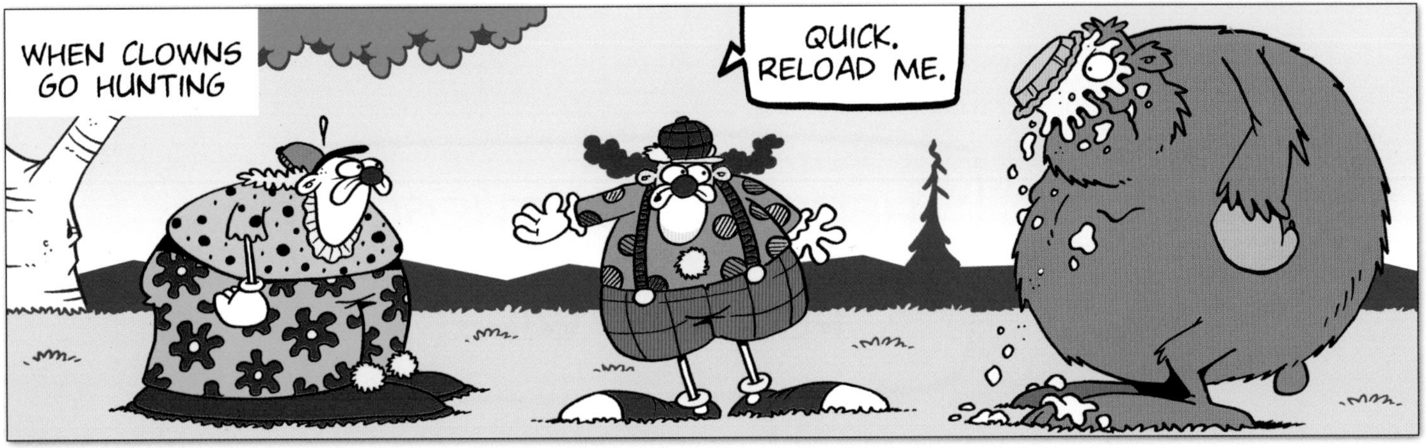
WHEN CLOWNS GO HUNTING
QUICK. RELOAD ME.

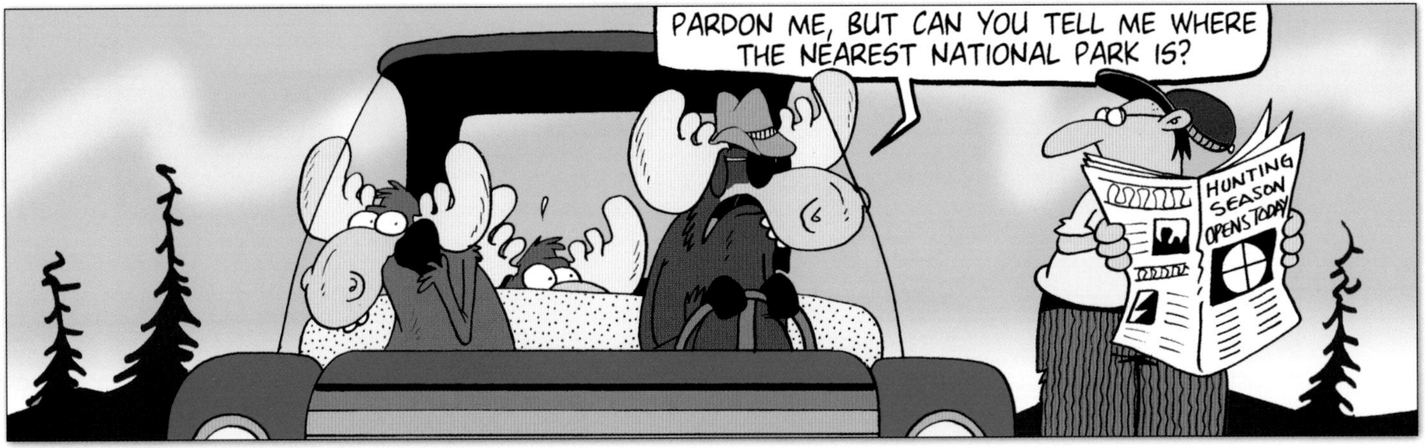
PARDON ME, BUT CAN YOU TELL ME WHERE THE NEAREST NATIONAL PARK IS?
HUNTING SEASON OPENS TODAY

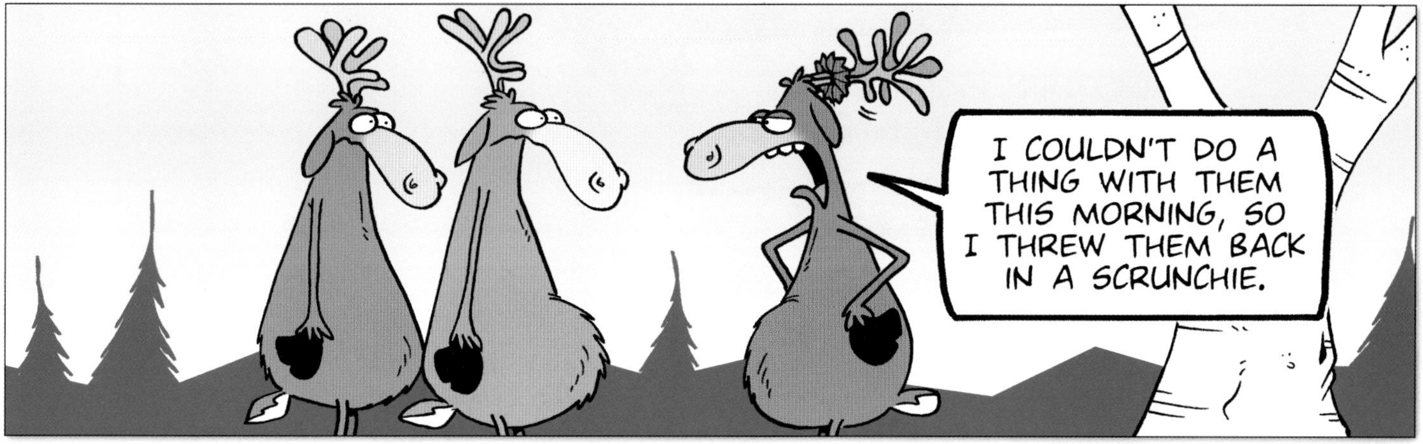
I COULDN'T DO A THING WITH THEM THIS MORNING, SO I THREW THEM BACK IN A SCRUNCHIE.

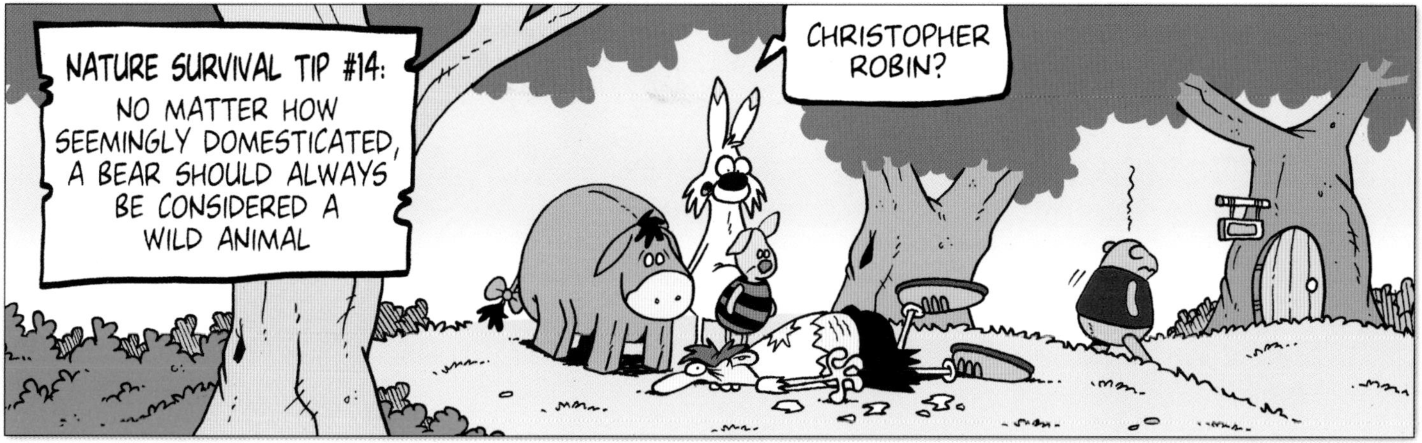
NATURE SURVIVAL TIP #14:
NO MATTER HOW SEEMINGLY DOMESTICATED, A BEAR SHOULD ALWAYS BE CONSIDERED A WILD ANIMAL
CHRISTOPHER ROBIN?

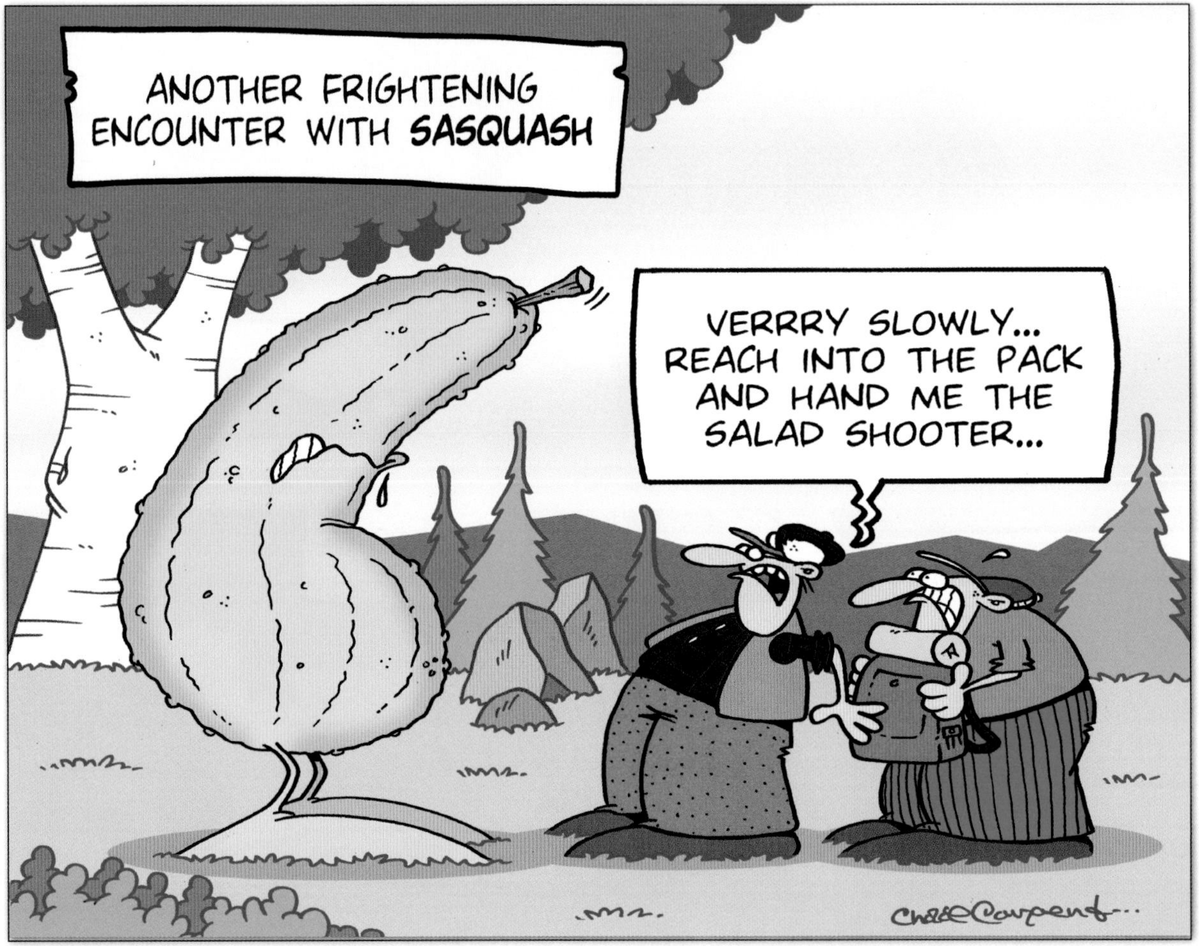
ANOTHER FRIGHTENING ENCOUNTER WITH SASQUASH
VERRRY SLOWLY... REACH INTO THE PACK AND HAND ME THE SALAD SHOOTER...

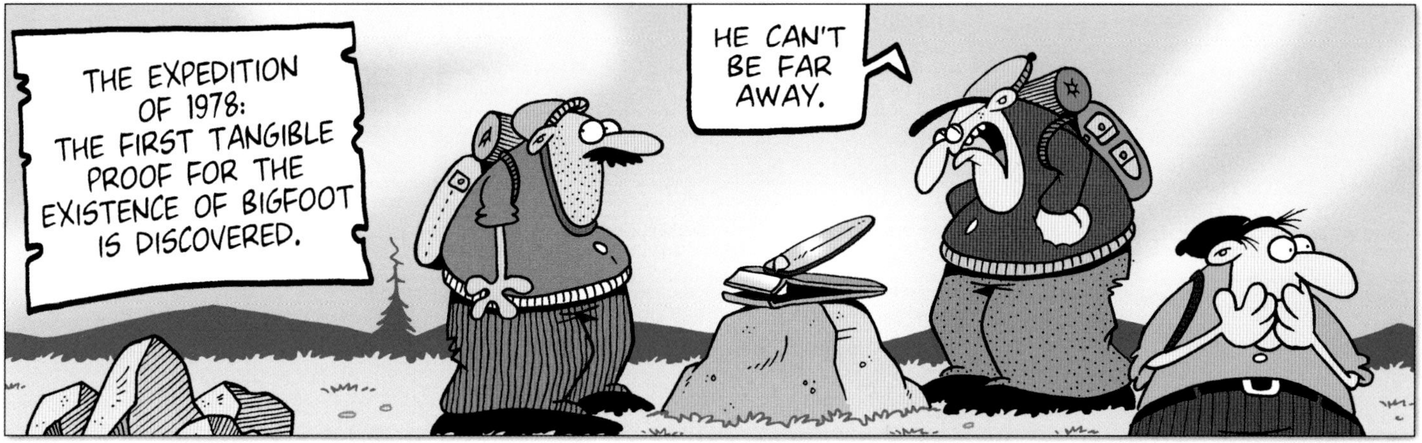
THE EXPEDITION OF 1978: THE FIRST TANGIBLE PROOF FOR THE EXISTENCE OF BIGFOOT IS DISCOVERED.
HE CAN'T BE FAR AWAY.

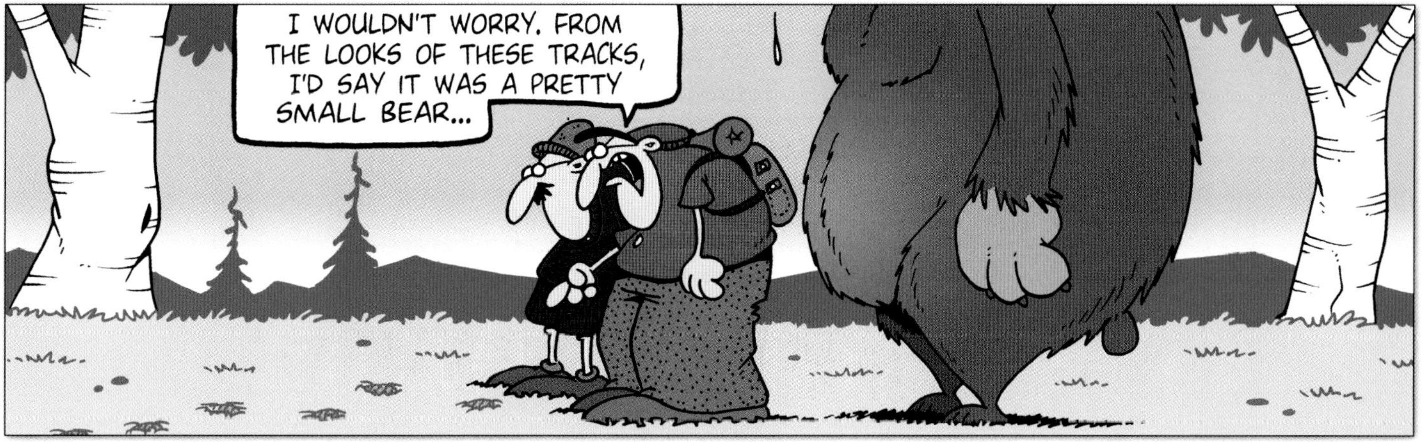
I WOULDN'T WORRY. FROM THE LOOKS OF THESE TRACKS, I'D SAY IT WAS A PRETTY SMALL BEAR...

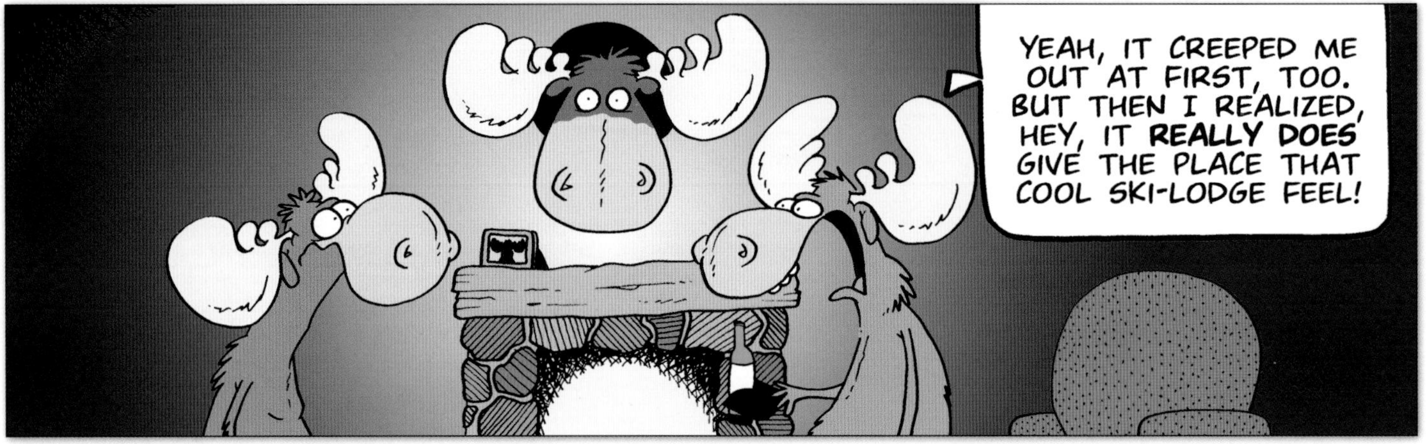
YEAH, IT CREEPED ME OUT AT FIRST, TOO. BUT THEN I REALIZED, HEY, IT **REALLY DOES** GIVE THE PLACE THAT COOL SKI-LODGE FEEL!

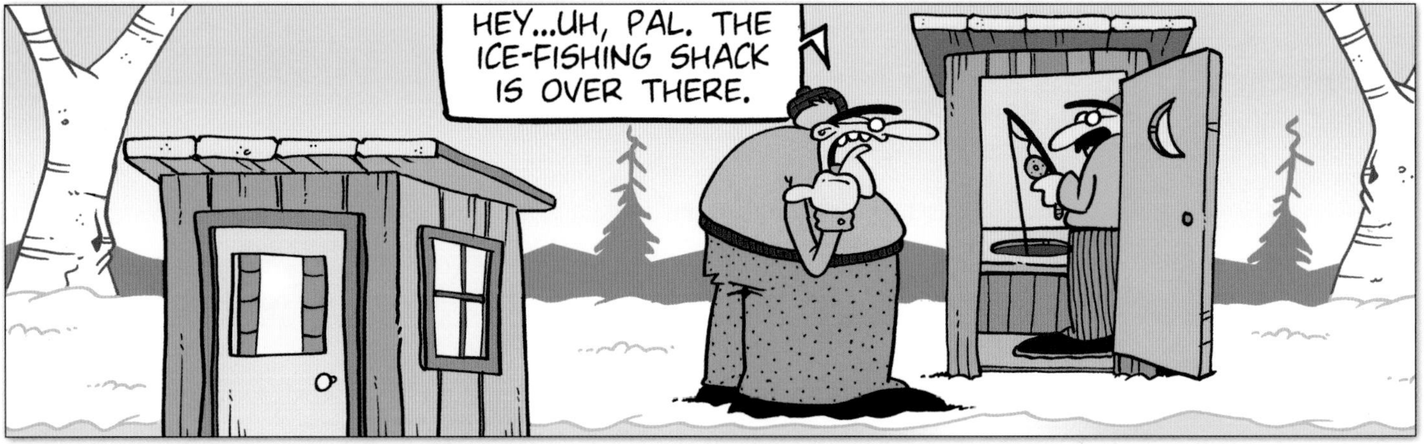
HEY...UH, PAL. THE ICE-FISHING SHACK IS OVER THERE.

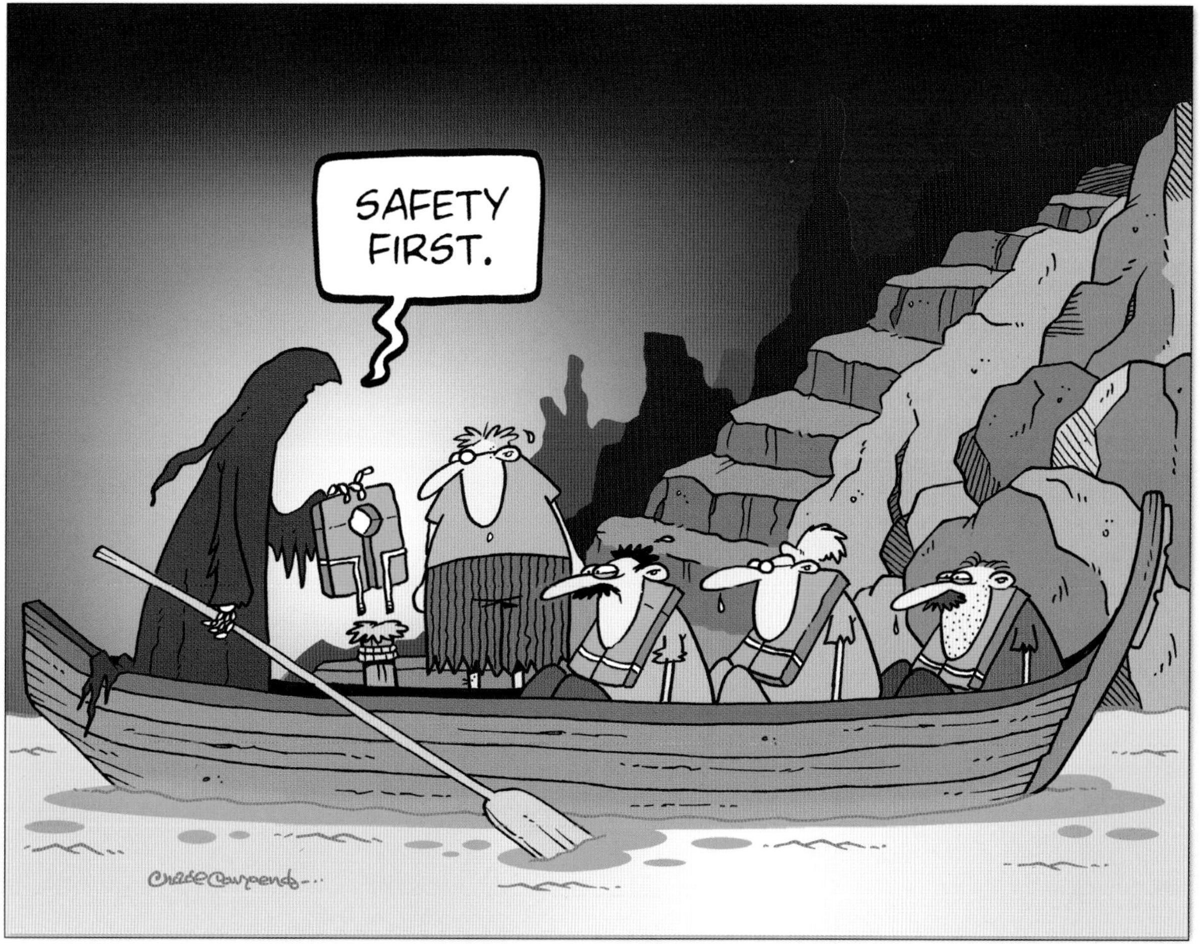
SAFETY FIRST.

The Official Short but Sweet Bio of Chad Carpenter

Having no other marketable talent, Chad decided to take a crack at a life-long ambition of being a newspaper cartoonist. The year was 1991 and he had just moved back to his home state of Alaska after living in Sarasota, Florida for three years. It was while in Sarasota that Chad became greatly inspired and personally advised by two of the comic strip greats - Mike Peters (Mother Goose & Grimm) & Dik Browne (Hagar the Horrible).

Shortly After arriving back in Alaska, armed with little more than 36 sample strips, a whole lot of ignorance and a burning desire to avoid real work, Chad went to the Anchorage Daily News to pedal his wares. The features editor took one look at "Tundra" and said "Eh, maybe we'll give it a try."

Fortunately, they actually did.

Shortly after the Daily News started running TUNDRA, it was picked up by most of the other Alaskan newspapers. A year later Chad was able to quit his job as a process server/security guard and devote all of his energy to being a cartoonist.

After 15 years of being only in Alaska newspapers, TUNDRA broke loose on the rest of the world.

In just five years, TUNDRA has added almost 500 newspapers including the L.A. Times, the Seattle Times, the Denver Post, the Pittsburgh Post, the San Francisco Chronicle as well as newspapers throughout Europe, Jamaica & Trinidad.

In May of 2008 Chad was presented with the Reuben Award for "Best Newspaper Panel" by the National Cartoonist Society.

Chad currently lives in Wasilla, Alaska with his wife Karen and four children. He is busy working on his 21st book as well as the latest calendars, shirts, greeting cards and anything else he can make a buck on.